BLACKOLOGY

THE THEOLOGICAL DEXTERITY OF BLACKNESS

YOEL OMOWALE

JEFF HOOD

FOR, NYOMI, MADELEINE, IMANI, JEFF, PHILLIP, QUINLEY & LUCAS...OUR CHILDREN...THAT THEY MIGHT ALL BE THEIR OWN BRILLIANT SHADES OF BLACK.

6

CONTENTS:

FOREWORD 10-17

INTRODUCTION 19-62

ATTRIBUTES OF BLACKNESS 64-116

THE TRINITY OF BLACKNESS 118-146

BLACK TRINITY DIALOGUE 149-169

THE BLACK PENTECOST. 172-190

ESCHATOLOGY 192-208

ESSAYS 210-352

THE BLACK BENEDICTION. 354

ESSAYS

WORDS FROM FERGUSON/ JEFF HOOD/ 212-218

AN EPISTLE TO THE CHURCH ON THE SEDUCTION OF WHITENESS INTO IDOLATRY/ YOEL OMOWALE / 220-253

BABEL / JEFF HOOD/ 255-266

THE FALL: *SOOT AND STENCH* / *YOEL OMOWALE*/ *268-343*

WHITE CHRISTIANS ARE THEOLOGICALLY COMPROMISED/ JEFF HOOD/ *345-352*

9

FOREWORD.

MAY 22, 2022

FELLOW SEEKERS.

"FUCK YOUR JESUS." AT FIRST, I JUST BLURTED IT OUT.

IN REALITY, I THINK IT WAS MORE OF A REFLEX. I

DIDN'T GO INTO THE ENCOUNTER EXPECTING IT TO GET THAT HEATED. I WASN'T THE FIERY TONGUED THEOLOGICAL ACTIVIST THAT I AM NOW. I WAS UPSET BUT NOT ENRAGED. IN FACT, I WAS ON MY BEST BEHAVIOR. I SIMPLY TOLD THE PRIEST THAT I THOUGHT THE HUGE STAINED-GLASS DEPICTION OF A WHITE JESUS WAS CONTRARY TO THE LOVING INCLUSIVE MESSAGE OF THE REAL JESUS. TO MY SURPRISE, SHE REPLIED, "WELL, THAT JESUS IS MY JESUS...AND MY JESUS IS THE REAL JESUS." SOMETHING CAME OVER ME. I LOST CONTROL. ZEAL FOR THE INCLUSIVE MESSAGE OF JESUS...THE LOVE OF

GOD...CONSUMED ME. I STARTED SAYING IT OVER AND OVER AGAIN, "FUCK YOUR JESUS." WHEN I WAS ASKED TO LEAVE, I KEPT SAYING IT, "FUCK YOUR JESUS." WHEN THEY STARTED PUSHING ME DOWN THE AISLE, I KEPT SAYING IT, "FUCK YOUR JESUS." WHEN THEY PUSHED ME OUT THE DOOR, I KEPT SAYING IT, "FUCK YOUR JESUS." WHEN THE DOOR SLAMMED BEHIND ME, I KEPT ON SAYING IT, "FUCK YOUR JESUS." WHEN ALL OF MY 'LIBERAL' FRIENDS CAME TO ME AND QUESTIONED MY APPROACH, I KEPT SAYING IT, "FUCK YOUR JESUS." HONESTLY, I DON'T KNOW WHEN I

STOPPED SAYING IT. BUT WHEN I DID, I HAD A VISION THAT HAS REMAINED WITH ME EVER SINCE.

THE PRIEST (I GUESS YOU COULD CALL HER KAREN) WAS STANDING IN FRONT OF THE GIGANTIC STAINED-GLASS DEPICTION OF A WHITE JESUS. I WAS STANDING ACROSS THE STREET WITH A COCONSPIRATOR. TOGETHER, WE WERE PRAYING WITH ALL OF OUR MIGHT THAT GOD WOULD COME DOWN AND DESTROY THIS ENORMOUS SYMBOL OF WHITE SUPREMACY. THEN, ALL OF A SUDDEN, A RUMBLING COMMENCED. THE REV. KAREN FELT IT TO. JUST AS SHE LOOKED UP,

THE FACE OF THE WHITE JESUS EXPLODED. GLASS WENT EVERYWHERE. MY COCONSPIRATOR AND I CHEERED. THE REV. KAREN COLLAPSED AND GRIEVED HER LOSS OF FAITH.

EVER SINCE I HAD THAT VISION, I HAVE MEASURED POTENTIAL COLLABORATORS BY IT. I WANT TO WORK WITH PEOPLE WHO WOULD JOIN ME...CHEERING...ACROSS THE STREET WHILE THE WHITE JESUS EXPLODED. WHEN I FOUNDED THE NEW THEOLOGY SCHOOL A NUMBER OF YEARS AGO, I DID SO WITH THE IDEA OF TRAINING AND FOSTERING community amongst people who were willing to stand up to the false gods of traditional religion...who were willing to boldly stand on the side of justice. In time, the community started to grow. In such a space, I met Dr. Yoel Omowale. After hearing his yearning for a world beyond white spirituality and all its' erasures, I knew I'd found a coconspirator. When we started talking about creating theology together, we constantly talked about what it would mean to make the world more colorful...not less. In our

CONVERSATIONS, IT BECAME APPARENT THAT GOD WAS DOING SOMETHING DIFFERENT. GOD SEEMED TO BE PROVIDING US WITH SOME DYNAMITE TO BLOW THE FACE OFF OF THE STAINED-GLASS JESUS. THE EXPLOSIVE RESULT IS THIS BOOK...BLACKOLOGY...A BEAUTIFUL THEOLOGICAL TREATISE OF A WORLD BEYOND THE WHITE JESUS...A WORLD MADE WHOLE BY COLOR.

TO ALL WHO WOULD QUESTION OUR AUDACITY TO CREATE SUCH A WORK...BASED ON ALL OF THEIR

ADDICTIONS TO THE WHITE JESUS…"FUCK YOUR JESUS."

THE REV. DR. JEFF HOOD

DEAN, THE NEW THEOLOGY SCHOOL

INTRODUCTION

IN THE BEGINNING, ALL WAS ***BLACK*** AS ***BLACKNESS*** ALREADY PRE-EXISTED. ***BLACKNESS*** WAS WITH "GOD", AND ***BLACKNESS*** WAS "GOD". GOD CREATED EVERYTHING THROUGH ***BLACKNESS***, AND NOTHING WAS CREATED EXCEPT THROUGH ***BLACKNESS***.

BLACKNESS GAVE LIFE TO EVERYTHING THAT WAS CREATED, AND THAT *BLACK*-BIRTHED LIFE BROUGHT LIGHT TO EVERYONE.

SELAH.

THE DRUMMER STRIKES UP A JAZZ RHYTHM IN A DIMLY LIT ROOM BREAKING THE NERVOUS SILENCE, THE DOUBLE BASS COMPLEMENTS THE ACCENTS AND KEEPS THE RECOGNIZABLE GROOVE, AND YOU ARE AT THE GLIMMERING, BLACK STEINWAY PIANO AT THE SMOKY BAR AND YOU GET TO IMPROVISE YOUR OWN

LIBERATIVE MELODY USING THE BLACK KEYS IN FRONT OF A SMALL CROWD PREGNANT WITH ANTICIPATION. WHAT DO YOU PLAY ROUN' MIDNIGHT TO CONJURE THE MAGIC IN THAT INTIMATE MOMENT? WHAT DOES THE BLACK NAKED SKY OUTSIDE INSPIRE YOU TO CREATE IN YOUR MIND THAT TRANSLATES TO YOUR FINGERS? WHERE IS GOD AND WHERE ARE WE IN ALL OF THIS TALK OF BLACKNESS? IT IS OFTEN FELT THAT ALL OF WHICH EXISTS COMES FROM NOTHING, BUT WHAT IS NOTHING? PERHAPS ALL SEEN AND UNSEEN ARE SIMPLY VARYING RESONANCES OF THE *BLACKNESS* THAT PRECEDED ALL THAT IS. MAYBE IT'S

NOT ENOUGH TO SAY WE ARE FROM THE BLACKNESS, OR THAT GOD IS BLACK WHICH HAS BEEN ARGUED TO BE TRUE. BUT WHAT IF THE VERY BLACKNESS FROM WHICH ALL THINGS EMERGED IS NOT JUST THE GROUND OF ALL BEING BUT THE VERY ESSENCE OF GOD?

SIMPLY PUT, WHAT IF THE *BLACKNESS* OF ALL ISNESS IS GOD?

THESE OPENING WORDS MAY HAVE OFFENDED YOUR RELIGIOUS SENSIBILITIES, PERHAPS IT HAS PIQUED your curiosity.   Humans make meaning - the why of what is, in the passion and creativity of life.   In what ways have these words triggered your imagination to contemplate the meaning making opportunities concerning conceptual *blackness?* In what ways might it challenge your current assumptions and presumptions of who God is, who we are, and what are we to do to thrive? We are creatures that are beholden to the quest of meaning- making as we engage the enchanting and sometimes overwhelming world around us.   The

VASTNESS OF THE MOSTLY BLACK UNIVERSE, BLOOMING WITH UNENDING BIOLOGICAL DIVERSITY IN ONE SMALL CORNER, THE INEXPLICABLE EMOTIONAL HIGHS AND DEVASTATING LOWS OF THE HUMAN EXPERIENCE, COMPELS US TO INTERROGATE, DECIPHER AND COMPOSE THE DEEPER SIGNIFICANCE OF IT ALL INTO OUR OWN SEMANTIC IMPROVISATION. THEOLOGY HAS BEEN A BROAD ROAD WELL-TRODDEN IN SEEKING TO MAKE SENSE AND ORIENT THE PURSUIT OF MEANING, BUT OFTEN WITHIN THE BOUNDARIES OF A PARTICULAR RELIGIOUS PARADIGM, GATE KEPT BY ORTHODOXY.   AS AN INFORMAL STUDENT OF theology over the years we found ourselves enjoying the intellectual engagement of its logic. It felt more akin to engaging ideas about God and the world like playing published sheet music - written by others for us to memorize and regurgitate. But the opportunity that grabbed a hold of me, and one that we think you should seriously consider joining us on, is improvising a new melody using the ingredients available to me, a melody that harmonizes uniquely with what went before with areas of tension and release.

Professor Anthony Pinn, Agnes Cullen Arnold Professor of Humanities and Professor of Religious Studies at Rice University, defined religion in much of his scholarly work as an embodied quest for complex subjectivity, or a push for more life meaning and we believe that useful theology must serve the body, mind and soul with the language and tools to pursue the rhythm and melody of that mission. The rhythm and improvised melody of this quest thus implies this journey is an innovative symphony on previously composed

FOUNDATIONS. UNFORTUNATELY, MUCH OF WESTERN PROTESTANT THEOLOGY IS A CULT OF DISEMBODIED ABSTRACTION THAT POISONS THE BODY AS THE SOURCE OF OUR CARNALITY AND NOTHING MORE THAN A HINDRANCE TO SPIRITUAL PURITY. IT'S IRONIC THAT A CENTRAL GOAL OF THAT THEOLOGICAL CORPUS IS ARTICULATING THE PLACE AND HOPE OF THE REDEEMED WITHIN THE BRUTALIZED BUT RESURRECTED BODY OF CHRIST, YET IS OFTEN SO PREJUDICED AGAINST THE NEEDS, DESIRES, BEAUTY AND PROPHETIC INSIGHTS OF THE BLACK AND OTHERWISE OPPRESSED BODY. WE HAVE SET OUT TO

CONSTRUCT, PERHAPS COMPOSE A SYSTEMATIC THEOLOGY THAT STARTS WITH THE CLOSEST BODY THAT WE KNOW, THE ONE WE HAVE FULL AUTONOMY OVER, FOR THEOLOGY MUST BE GROUNDED IN WHAT IS CORPORAL AND UNDOUBTEDLY ALIVE. OURSACRED *BLACK* BODY.

MY BODY IS ANIMATED *BLACKNESS*, IT IS ALIVE BECAUSE OF THAT PRIMORDIAL BLACKNESS AFOREMENTIONED IN WHICH WE LIVE, MOVE AND HAVEOURBEING.   IT THEREFORE ISN'T SOMETHING WE CAN DIVEST OF WHEN UNDERSTOOD IN THIS WAY, IT IS inherent and inseparably what we am substantiated by.

Once you name a work as a theological endeavor, questions that may naturally occur could include.   What religion or ideology is this in aid of? To what authority, revelation or tradition does it appeal? These questions are important and especially so within the normative way we engage classical theology.   What we aspire to achieve in this work is expand the scope, possibilities and reach of theology into innovative territory, that invites the reader from any background, well-read in theology or not, religious or otherwise, to discover something new about making life-transforming meaning out of our shared humanity in Blackness. Theology is said to be built on revelation, that which we engage as a lens to explicate this deeper meaning and significance of life. The revelation of this theological endeavor is *Blackness* itself. This might seem a bold proposition to some, idolatrous to others or frankly untenable, but we hope to present a case for why we believe *blackness* is holy ground, and a suitable substrate upon which to grapple with the complexity of life. The underpinning idea of this theological treatise is that *blackness* is the pre-eminent reality that pre-exists all things, through which all things were made and it was all good. This is what we mean by *blackology*. It was all *black* in the beginning. Many have contemplated God being black. In 1966, anti-apartheid US Senator Robert F. Kennedy who was later assassinated in Los Angeles, famously asked the question in response to the ill-treatment of Black Americans and South Africans, "But suppose God is Black? What if we go to Heaven and we, all our lives, have treated the Negro as an inferior, and God is there, and we look up and He is not white? What then is our response?" (Look Magazine, "Suppose God is

BLACK," BY SEN. ROBERT F. KENNEDY. AUG. 23, 1966).

THE QUESTION CHALLENGED HIS WHITE, SELF-IDENTIFIED CHRISTIAN LISTENERS WHO LARGELY SAW THEIR WHITENESS AS AN INHERENTLY SUPERIOR, DIVINELY ENDOWED CHARACTERISTIC, AND HE CONNECTED THE DOTS IN THAT SIMPLE STATEMENT OF THE PRE-SUPPOSED WHITENESS OF GOD THAT UNDERPINNED THEIR CONVICTIONS. BUT GIVEN WHAT WE HAVE SAID SO FAR ABOUT THE BLACKNESS THAT WAS PRE-EXISTENT, THE WHITENESS OF GOD IS

UNTENABLE. THE BLACKNESS OF GOD IN SOME THEOLOGICAL DISCOURSE HAS SOMETIMES FELT LIKE A SKIN THING RATHER THAN A SUBSTANTIAL THING THAT ALL HUMANITY IS ALSO CO-SUBSTANTIVE WITH. FOR IF WE ARE IN FACT MADE IN THE IMAGE OF GOD AS THE JUDEO-CHRISTIAN TRADITION CLAIMS, WE ARE MADE OF THE SAME ESSENTIAL STUFF. THE *BLACKNESS* WE REFER TO IS RADICALLY INCLUSIVE BECAUSE IT ISN'T REDUCED TO A CULTURAL AESTHETIC THOUGH IT INCLUDES THAT, IT ISN'T LIMITED TO A RACIAL IDENTITY NOR THE SHADE OF ONE'S SKIN THOUGH IT ENCOMPASSES THAT. DARK MATTER, THE VERY STUFF

OF EXISTENCE, IS THOUGHT TO ACCOUNT FOR APPROXIMATELY 85% OF THE MATTER IN THE UNIVERSE. THERE IS AN ENLIGHTENING, ELECTRIFYING COMMUNAL AND SACRED REALITY LOCATED IN IDENTIFYING OUR SHARED BLACKNESS IN A METAPHYSICAL AND DARE WE SAY SPIRITUAL SENSE- ALL OF US, INCLUDING WHATEVER ONE IMAGINES AS GOD.

IT IS ALMOST NEEDLESS TO SAY THAT WE ABIDE A WORLD WHICH HAS VERY POLARIZING VIEWS OF HUMAN IDENTITY ESPECIALLY AS IT RELATES TO RACE,

RELIGION, GENDER AND SEXUALITY. THERE HAS BEEN A GREAT SCHISM IN SOCIETIES, PARTICULARLY IN THE WEST, ON THE HISTORIC ISSUE OF RACE AS A SOCIAL CONSTRUCT. SEVERAL CENTURIES OF WESTERN IMPERIALISM, ALIGNED WITH CHRISTIAN ENDORSEMENT AS THE STATE RELIGION, SOCIETIES WERE ORGANIZED INTO A HIERARCHY OF RACIAL CASTS WITH WORSENING LIFE PROSPECTS AND DARKER SKIN THE LO WE R DOWN THE SOCIAL LADDER ONE FOUND THEMSELVES. THIS PAINFUL LEGACY PERSISTS AND WHILE IN SOME WAYS THERE HAS BEEN LIMITED PROGRESS, AROUND THE WORLD ONE CAN find pervasive ways in which people are oppressed or experience negative social determinants due to one's *blackness*. It is in this cultural locus of "otherness", where there are unique experiences of suffering, angst and existential questions of which we can explore. In his riveting book *"Is God a White Racist?"* Rev. Dr. William Jones pitched the argument that theodicy is a necessary concept we must engage as we try to explore the meaning of black suffering at the hands of white delusions of supremacy. For if God is believed to be

SOVEREIGN OVER HUMAN HISTORY WHILE ABLE TO INTERVENE WHERE THERE IS PARTICULAR AND EGREGIOUS SUFFERING ON THE GROUNDS OF ONE'S *BLACKNESS,* THEN SOME FEEL HE IS CULPABLE. THERE IS AN URGENT SENSE OF A LIMITED OPPORTUNITY TO ADDRESS AN ANCIENT GLOBAL PANDEMIC OF *BLACK* PSYCHOSPIRITUAL DISEMPOWERMENT THROUGH A PERVASIVE AND CHRONIC PLAGUE OF ANTI-BLACKNESS. IT'S URGENT BECAUSE SINCE GEORGE FLOYD'S BRUTAL ROADSIDE EXECUTION, THERE WAS A WORLDWIDE RECKONING OF THE WAYS THAT PUBLIC SPECTACLE OF HIS DEATH SENT OUT AN SOS CALL

ABOUT THE VICIOUS CONSEQUENCES OF RACISM. WE ABIDE A WORLD WHERE PEOPLE LABELLED OR SELF-IDENTIFIED AS *'BLACK'*, OFTEN FIND THEMSELVES TRAPPED IN AN EXTERNALLY IMPOSED, LIMITING LATTICE OF EXISTENTIAL POSSIBILITIES. THESE DOMAINS INCLUDE BUT AREN'T LIMITED TO SOCIOECONOMIC DISENFRANCHISEMENT, POLITICAL UNDERREPRESENTATION AND SPIRITUAL HOPELESSNESS. RACE, GENDER, CLASS, RELIGION AND SEXUALITY INTERFACE WITH LABYRINTHINE COMPLEXITY TO NUANCE HOW BLACK DISEMPOWERMENT MANIFESTS BUT THERE SEEMS TO BE insufficient universal resources to broadly and directly address the deep spiritual malaise that underpins the varying symptoms. There is a pervasive discomfort within for many who have witnessed faith fashioned into a spear and hurled at those on the margins of a society. You might be feeling that discomfort right now as you read this introduction.

How do we devotionally reflect on the meaning derived and impact of our faith-based assumptions, beliefs, and actions to hopefully arrive at a way of faith and living that provides safety to those on the margins and disrupts the status quo? How will that discomfort you might currently feel motivate you theologically? That is what we hope this book can begin to offer its readers. But this is more than an intellectual project of decolonization, for the redemption of Blackness is not purely relative to the project of European imperialism. We would like to reconfigure the project of theologizing Blackness as developing a new spiritual imagination with its own origin story. We want to invite you, the reader, to imagine the possibilities of your own spiritual transformation by engaging in this work. Regardless of what you believe religiously, what your race, nationality, gender or sexuality is, *Blackology* presents a radically inclusive opportunity to take what has been universally scorned and killed and use it to resurrect a collective destiny of liberation possibilities.

BEFORE WE GO MUCH FURTHER, WE WANT TO SPECIFICALLY ADDRESS CHRISTIANS HERE IN SAYING THAT WE ARE PAST THE POINT OF NO RETURN CONCERNING THE CULTURAL BANKRUPTCY OF ENGAGING HOLISTIC *BLACKNESS* IN POPULAR CHRISTIAN THEOLOGY AND PRAXIS. MUCH OF THE WAY CHRISTIANITY IS PRACTICED IN THE WEST BARRICADES OR DE-PRIORITIZES INDIGENOUS EXPRESSION AND LIBERATION THROUGH WESTERN CULTURAL AND MORAL IMPERIALISM. WE ARE MOSTLY BLIND TO IT, THINKING THAT THE HISTORIC THEOLOGIES WE'VE INHERITED ARE CULTURALLY

NEUTRAL. WE ARE SO ENTRENCHED IN COLONIZED ASSUMPTIONS ABOUT FAITH TO THE POINT WHERE WE SEE THE PROJECT OF DECOLONIZATION AS INHERENTLY UNCHRISTIAN. OUR UNDERSTANDING OF SIN IS EXCESSIVELY FOCUSED ON WHAT WE ARE PROHIBITED FROM DOING CONSENSUALLY BETWEEN TWO UNMARRIED ADULTS IN THE BEDROOM, AT THE GRAVE OMISSION OF THE INFRASTRUCTURAL EVILS THAT PERPETUATE THE GREATEST HUMAN SUFFERING. SADLY, WE OFTEN SEE MORE CHRIST-LIKE CHARACTER FROM THOSE WHO DON'T ASCRIBE TO RITUALS, PRIORITIES, DOCTRINES, AND POLITICS OF WESTERN

CHRISTIANITY. THIS HAS MOTIVATED US TO STUDY OUR UNIVERSAL FAITH TRADITION MORE CLOSELY, SEPARATING THE MEAT FROM BONES, SO WE CAN CREATE SOME DISTANCE FROM THE WESTERN ASSUMPTIONS ABOUT CHRIST. IT IS OUR CONTENTION THAT WITH THAT CONSCIOUSNESS, BLACK BODIES WOULD BE ABLE TO LIVE AND THRIVE MORE AUTHENTICALLY AND FREELY AS A HUMAN BEING LET ALONE A PERSON OF FAITH. FOR THERE IS TOO MUCH PRETENSE IN COLONIZED SPIRITUALITY. PART OF THE WORK OF BLACK THEOLOGY IS IN EXPLORING OUR INTUITIVE IMPRESSIONS OF

BLACKNESS AND ALL IT REPRESENTS SOCIALLY, POLITICALLY, EVEN SEXUALLY, AS A LENS FOR THEOLOGICAL INQUIRY.

HOW COMFORTABLE DO YOU FEEL WITH THE THEOLOGICAL UTILITY OF BLACKNESS?

ON THE CONVERSE, BLACK THEOLOGY DEMANDS THAT WE EXAMINE OUR RELATIONSHIP WITH WHITENESS AS A HERMENEUTIC TO ESTABLISH THE VERACITY AND SUPERIORITY OF A SPIRITUAL IDEA, RITUAL OR PRAXIS.

Are we trapped within the logic of whiteness obligated to vilify, exploit and appropriate expressions of blackness?

Every aspect of our faith journeys have taught us something we needed to learn about our complete divine self that is synthesizing our unique theological *innerstanding.*

Prof Anthony Reddie, Extraordinary Professor of Theological Ethics at the

University of South Africa (Black Religion and Aesthetics: Religious Thought and Life in Africa and the African Diaspora / edited by Anthony B. Pinn), used the function of improvisation in jazz to illustrate the creative opportunity of theological innovation by stating:

"The art of improvisation is a challenge to find new meaning and phrases to transform an existing melody, without departing from the original to such an extent that the previous incarnation is obliterated. In effect, it is the

delicate synthesis of bringing the new from the old—bearing witness to what has gone before, but not being limited or constrained by it."

What we intend to do with this work we've defined as a systematic *Blackology*, is to interrogate various sources to innovate and articulate a comprehensive, systematic

THEOLOGY OF BLACKNESS THAT HAS THE FOLLOWING ATTRIBUTES:

UNIVERSAL - WHILE WE USE THE TERM THEOLOGY TO DESCRIBE THIS TREATISE, IT IS BY NO MEANS LIMITED TO THEISTIC NOTIONS OF SPIRITUALITY NOR ANY PARTICULAR RELIGIOUS DOGMA. WE WILL DRAW ON A PLETHORA OF SOURCES FOR INSPIRATION. THIS ATTRIBUTE ALSO SPEAKS TO THE INTERNATIONAL SCOPE OF THIS WORK AS THERE ARE MANY BLACK THEOLOGIES THAT ARE PARTICULAR TO JUST A US-CENTRIC PERSPECTIVE THAT MAY NOT SPEAK AS

POTENTLY TO BLACKNESS IN OTHER CULTURAL SPACES. WE WILL ATTEMPT TO HIGHLIGHT INSIGHTS WHICH AREN'T OFTEN REPRESENTED. WE REALLY HOPE THIS WORK PARTICULARLY MAKES LIBERATIVE THEOLOGY MORE HUMANISTIC AND WHILE DRAWING ON THE INSIGHTS AND CONCEPTS OF ACADEMIC DISCOURSE, WE WANT THIS WORK TO BE ACCESSIBLE BEYOND THE WALLS OF THE ACADEMY.

LIBERATIVE - THE PURPOSE OF THIS WORK IS TO PROVIDE A RE-SYNTHESIZED THEOLOGICAL FRAMEWORK TO RE-IMAGINE, REDEEM, AND ultimately liberate Black embodied people from the aforementioned psycho-spiritual bondage they experience in its manifold manifestations. But as mentioned above and we hasten to re-emphasize, there is a universal redemptive opportunity in locating our shared humanity, by choosing to incarnate our personal sense of being into a communal amalgamation of Blackness. This is not an appropriation of Blackness for those not considered socially Black but rather a humbling and mutual synergistic incarnation

FOR THE PURPOSE OF LIBERATION FROM THE MAN-MADE CURSE OF ANTI-BLACKNESS.

IMAGINATIVE - THIS WORK WANTS TO GIVE THOSE WHO ENGAGE A KIND OF MAGIC AND MYSTIQUE IN WHICH TO GROUND THE BEAUTY OF BLACKNESS, IT IS NOT MERELY INTELLECTUAL LABOR, BUT AN OPPORTUNITY TO CULTIVATE A KIND OF ROBUST basis for Black mysticism that empowers the Black mind, soul and body unto salvation.

It must be stated that we are very aware of the scholarly work of Black liberation, womanist and queer theologies that have preceded this work, from which we have drawn significant influence and inspiration. We will be drawing on these legacies throughout this work and hopefully using ingredients from a variety of sources to synthesize something novel but resonant with those traditions.

In the first chapter we will present the doctrine of *blackness* nestled in its own reimagined origin story, then expounding on it's attributes and their wider implications. This will set a foundation to build a hermeneutic for engaging the deep questions of otherness often felt about blackness in certain social contexts, but will simultaneously construct a redemptive model of conceptual Blackness to aspire towards.

In the second chapter we'd like to unpack what we consider the Trinity of Blackness - *Blackbody, Blackmind, Blacksoul.* These categories aren't novel, comprehensive nor exclusive to any other aspect of Blackness at the physical or metaphysical level, but they provide a definitive framework to conceptualize the challenges, threats, solutions and hopes of Blackness in a holistic,

INTEGRATIVE MANNER. THIS EXPLICIT USE OF THE CHRISTIAN TERM TRINITY SPEAKS TO THE NOTION THAT EACH CATEGORY IS SUFFICIENTLY DISTINCT, NEEDING ACKNOWLEDGEMENT OF ITS PARTICULAR FUNCTION AND FOCUS, YET ARE CO-EQUAL IN IMPORTANCE AND CO-SUBSTANTIVE IN DEFINING BLACKNESS.

IN THE THIRD CHAPTER, WE AIM TO ENGAGE THE IDEA OF A BLACK PENTECOST. THIS IS PUSHING INTO THE IDEA THAT A BLACK GOD OR BLACKNESS ITSELF IS RESCUING THE WORLD FROM ANTI-BLACKNESS.

There is a beautiful diaspora taking place all around us. New words...thoughts...ideas...music...and a variety of other Black expressions are exploding all around us. The meaning of shared Black love and it's promise for the future is found here.

In the final chapter, defined as a *Black* *Eschatology*, we will attempt to reimagine hope through the lens of Black ontological realities. Hope as a vision that is being materialized. The only one we know

DEFINITIVELY WE HAVE TO GUIDE US FORWARD.

BLACKNESS HAS REVEALED TO US WHAT IS COMING.

LISTEN TO THE FUTURE.

IN CLOSING, WE ARE REMINDED OF ONE OF OUR FAVORITE QUOTES BY CRITICALLY ACCLAIMED AUTHOR, JAMES BALDWIN:

"MOST OF US, NO MATTER WHAT WE SAY, ARE WALKING IN THE DARK, WHISTLING IN THE DARK. NOBODY KNOWS WHAT IS GOING TO HAPPEN TO HIM FROM ONE MOMENT TO THE NEXT, OR HOW ONE WILL

BEAR IT. THIS IS IRREDUCIBLE. AND IT'S TRUE OF EVERYBODY. NOW, IT IS TRUE THAT THE NATURE OF SOCIETY IS TO CREATE, AMONG ITS CITIZENS, AN ILLUSION OF SAFETY; BUT IT IS ALSO ABSOLUTELY TRUE THAT THE SAFETY IS ALWAYS NECESSARILY AN ILLUSION. ARTISTS ARE HERE TO DISTURB THE PEACE."

FOR AS BALDWIN WAS ALSO KNOWN TO HAVE SAID WHICH RINGS TRUE TO THE KIND OF CHANGE WE HOPE THIS WORK STIMULATES,

"ANY REAL CHANGE IMPLIES THE BREAKUP OF THE WORLD AS ONE HAS ALWAYS KNOWN IT, THE LOSS OF ALL THAT GAVE ONE AN IDENTITY, THE END OF SAFETY."

WE HOPE YOU FIND THIS WORK STIMULATING AND PROVOCATIVE, AT TIMES YOU MAY FEEL OFFENDED, BUT DO REMEMBER THAT THE INTENT OF THIS PROJECT IS THAT WE CAN ALL LOCATE OURSELVES METAPHYSICALLY IN THIS COLLECTIVE WORK OF LIBERATION, BY HUMBLING SELF-EXAMINATION AND

FAITHFUL APPLICATION IN AUTHENTIC COMMUNITY. THIS JOURNEY WE ARE ABOUT TO EMBARK ON TOGETHER WILL HOPEFULLY STIR UP GOOD TROUBLE, BUT *BLACKNESS* IS NOT SHY IN THE STATEMENT OF ITS PERENNIAL MISSION, **BLACK IS GOD!**

63

THE DOCTRINE OF BLACKNESS - ATTRIBUTES

IT'S BEEN SO LONG INSIDE THIS PLACE THAT WE'VE LOST COUNT OF THE TIME AND A PERCEPTION OF SPACE.   IT'S WET, WARM AND PITCH BLACK.   THERE IS A KIND OF QUIET SAFETY THAT WE'VE BECOME ACCLIMATED TO, PROTECTED WITHIN WHAT APPEARS

TO BE SOLITARY CONFINEMENT. IN THIS BLACKNESS WE'RE NOURISHED, FORTIFIED AND SHAPED BUT WE'RE UNAWARE OF THE SOURCE OF THIS INTENTIONAL CARE. THERE'S AN ENERGY WITHIN THIS DARKNESS THAT SUSTAINS AND DIRECTS US, INCUBATING OUR BODIES, MINDS AND SOULS, WHICH HAVE BEGUN TO PERCEIVE THE PREMONITIONS OF CATACLYSMIC CHANGE. WE START TO NOTICE FLASHES OF LUMINOUS BEAMS, WE TASTE THE WARM FLUID THAT ENCASES US, WE FEEL THE PULSATING LIFE PENETRATING US AS WE DRIFT IN AND OUT OF SLEEP. STARTLING SOUNDS AND VIBRATIONS TRANSMITTED from the outside world echo inside, carried by the waves and begin to disturb the peace within. The pressure inside intensifies as it prepares for imminent evacuation. The deep waters break with a loud explosion and gush forth, draining our aquarian home and we emerge gasping for air for the first time, in the most blinding light we've ever seen, and we're nestled in the arms of our creators.

Blackness is the primordial reality in which all existential potentiality resides, and by which the universe and all its life are incubated, sustained and birthed. Even the conception of the human embryo, occurs when one lucky sperm from the pack fertilizes the ovum in the darkness, and is formed, shaped and nourished in the darkness.

It's within the context of darkness that light and life are discerned and defined. Blackness however has often been characterized negatively as the utter absence of light in both a natural and metaphorical sense. However definitions and their assumptions belong to the definers, not to the defined; and part of the work of theology is to interrogate the definition of concepts we often take for granted.

In order to understand what blackness constitutes as it relates to human identity, it's necessary to explore the ways blackness translates in our collective psyche and imagination. The creative imagination of Western culture tends to portray black as symbolic of evil, with almost every villain one can readily think of being painted as ominous with dark features. Blackness is often interpreted as unclean and unsightly, suspicious yet strangely exotic. For this reason blackness often performs the trope of the indulgent guilty pleasure, the object of exotic fantasy and perilous fetishization.

Philosopher Lewis Gordon argued that ontological reflection on the existential meaning of blackness requires attention to the concrete actuality of the situated moments of

Black suffering (The Oxford Handbook of African American Theology, Katie G. Cannon, Anthony B. Pinn, 2014). In other words, we can't ignore the exact locations of how blackness is imagined, embodied and experienced when attempting to engage what it means unless you are dealing in pure abstraction.

Across six studies, people used a "bad is black" heuristic in social judgment and assumed that immoral acts were committed by people with

DARKER SKIN TONES, REGARDLESS OF THE RACIAL BACKGROUND OF THOSE IMMORAL ACTORS (THE "BAD IS BLACK" EFFECT: WHY PEOPLE BELIEVE EVILDOERS HAVE DARKER SKIN THAN DO-GOODERS, ADAM L. ALTER, CHADLY STERN, YAEL GRANOT). IN WESTERN CULTURE, BLACK HAS BEEN A SYMBOL FOR DEATH, MOURNING, SIN & EVIL, AND THE STRANGE OR THE "OTHER" IN WRITING AND LITERATURE.

THE INTERNAL DISDAIN MANY FEEL ABOUT BLACKNESS IS ALSO OFTEN CULTURALLY INDOCTRINATED AND TRAUMATIC, WITH COMPELLING REMINDERS

EVERYWHERE THAT THEY BELIEVE RIGHTLY. THIS FALSELY BELIEVED INFERIORITY OF "BLACKNESS" IS ONE OF THE UNDERPINNING NARRATIVES OF WESTERN INTELLECTUAL ENGAGEMENT. SOME MAY FEEL THIS PREJUDICED VIEW OF BLACKNESS IS TOO DEEPLY INGRAINED INTO OUR COLLECTIVE PSYCHE AND ANY EFFORT TO DIVEST FROM THIS A FUTILE ENDEAVOR. WE DISAGREE AND IT IS FOR THIS REASON WE BELIEVE THE FIRST TASK AT HAND IS TO INTERROGATE, THEN RECONSIDER BLACKNESS WITH AN ALTERNATIVE CREATIVE IMAGINATION THAT SUBVERTS THIS HISTORICAL NARRATIVE. WE USE THE TERM doctrine with some crucial caveats. Definitionally, a doctrine is a belief or set of beliefs held and taught by a church, political party, or other group. The ideas we're about to articulate as a doctrine of blackness are not beholden to any particular church, religion, ideology or ethnic nationalism. These ideas are also open to scrutiny and further refinement through dialectical engagement with varying sources. Prof Anthony Reddie argued that black religion and its resultant spiritualities was one where the listener was inspired by tales of another mythic world and that the power of inspired oratory transported the listener to "another space and time." (Theologising Brexit: A Liberationist and Postcolonial Critique, Anthony G. Reddie, 2019). Therefore, we intend to expound an origin story of Blackness that supersedes any human invention at the conceptual level, in another space and time, which we think helps to firmly route it in nature and something we can all understand and engage at some level irrespective of our

METAPHYSICAL COMMITMENTS. WE INVITE YOU TO READ THE FOLLOWING BRIEF PASSAGES AND REFLECT ON HOW THEY CHALLENGE YOUR BELIEF ABOUT BLACKNESS.

IN THE BEGINNING, ALL WAS BLACK AS **BLACKNESS** ALREADY PRE-EXISTED.

BLACKNESS WAS WITH "GOD", AND **BLACKNESS** WAS "GOD". GOD CREATED EVERYTHING THROUGH **BLACKNESS**, AND NOTHING WAS CREATED EXCEPT THROUGH **BLACKNESS**. **BLACKNESS** GAVE LIFE TO

EVERYTHING THAT WAS CREATED, AND THAT **BLACK** BIRTHED LIFE BROUGHT LIGHT TO EVERYONE.

INSPIRED BY JOHN 1:1

IN THE BEGINNING GOD CREATED THE HEAVENS AND THE EARTH. THE EARTH WAS FORMLESS AND EMPTY, AND **DARKNESS** COVERED THE DEEP WATERS. AND THE SPIRIT OF GOD WAS HOVERING OVER THE SURFACE OF THE WATERS.

GENESIS 1:1-2

The Book of the Dead, dating to the Second Intermediate Period, describes how the world was created by Atum, the god of Heliopolis, the centre of the sun-god cult in Lower Egypt. In the beginning, the world appeared as an infinite expanse of dark and directionless waters, named

NUN.

ATTRIBUTE 1 - PRE-EXISTENT DIVINITY

RACE AS A CATEGORIZING TERM REFERRING TO HUMAN BEINGS WAS FIRST USED IN THE ENGLISH LANGUAGE IN THE LATE 16TH CENTURY. UNTIL THE 18TH CENTURY IT HAD A GENERALIZED MEANING SIMILAR TO OTHER CLASSIFYING TERMS SUCH AS TYPE, SORT, OR KIND. BY THE 18TH CENTURY, RACE WAS WIDELY USED FOR SORTING AND RANKING THE PEOPLES IN THE ENGLISH COLONIES—EUROPEANS who saw themselves as free people, indigenous persons who had been conquered, and Africans who were being brought in as slave labor—and this usage continues today. Toward the end of the 17th century, labor from England began to diminish, and the colonies faced the dilemma of how to obtain a controllable labor force as cheaply as possible. Tobacco was the chief source of wealth, and its production was labor-intensive. The colonial leaders found a solution by the 1690s they had divided the

RESTLESS POOR INTO CATEGORIES REFLECTING THEIR

ORIGINS, HOMOGENIZING ALL EUROPEANS INTO A

"WHITE" CATEGORY AND INSTITUTING A SYSTEM OF

PERMANENT SLAVERY FOR AFRICANS AS THE "BLACK" CATEGORY.

BLACKNESS IN THE ANTHROPOLOGICAL SENSE, AS A RACIAL CATEGORY RELATIVE TO SOLVING THE EUROPEAN LABOR PROBLEM WAS BORN.

BUT THIS WAS NOT THE ORIGIN STORY OF BLACKNESS.

PRIOR TO THIS, WHILE RACE DIDN'T EXIST IN THE SAME WAY AS DEFINED BY EUROPEANS, THE LAND OF ANCIENT KEMET WAS SO CALLED BECAUSE OF THE DARK COMPLEXION OF ITS INHABITANTS THOUSANDS of years before later European civilizations emerged. More importantly, there needs to be greater recognition that *blackness* is not a solution to a white problem but is pre-existent to whiteness itself. This creates a vision of

BLACKNESS THAT ISN'T SUBSERVIENT TO WHITENESS IN ANY WAY AND TIES INTO THE NEXT ATTRIBUTE.

HERE WE ESTABLISH THE PRIMACY OF BLACKNESS AS A PRE-EMINENT REALITY INSPIRED BY THE POETIC LANGUAGE OF JOHN 1:1.

*IN THE BEGINNING, ALL WAS **BLACK** AS **BLACKNESS** ALREADY PRE-EXISTED.*

BLACKNESS IS BEING ANCHORED AT THE BEGINNING OF THE BEGINNING AND THE VERY NATURE OF THE

UNIVERSE AFFIRMS THE PERVASIVE, TIMELESS AND LIMITLESS EXPANSE OF BLACKNESS.

IN THE OPENING BIBLICAL TEXT OF GENESIS 1:1 DETAILING THE CREATION STORY, WE SEE AN ALLEGORICAL DEPICTION OF THE PRIMACY OF BLACKNESS, THAT COVERED THE DEEP WATERS OVER WHICH GOD HOVERS AT THE ORIGIN OF THAT PARTICULAR CREATION STORY.

AGAIN IT MUST BE CLARIFIED, THE PURPOSE OF USING THESE SCRIPTURAL TEXTS ISN'T TO CLAIM THEM AS truths in a literal sense, nor argue about what they mean in an absolute sense, but to provide a metaphysical substrate upon which to ground the mystery of blackness as part of the first cause of all things conceptually.   Even the creation account in the Book of the Dead, we

SEE THE WORLD WAS PRE-EXISTENT AS DARK, STILL, INFINITE WATERS.

IN THE POEM MELANIN BY NAYYIRAH WAHEED FROM HER BOOK NEJMA REFERENCED ABOVE, SHE BEAUTIFULLY SAYS THESE LINES:

MELANIN.

IS THE WORLD.   BEFORE THIS WORLD.

BEFORE THE WORD.   SLAVE.

IN REFERENCING MELANIN, THE PIGMENT THAT DARKENS THE SKIN THAT ALL HUMANS SHARE TO VARYING DEGREES, SHE ARTICULATES ITS TOTAL DIGNITY AS *THE WORLD* AND IT'S ORIGIN BEFORE *THIS WORLD* WHERE IT'S DIGNITY WAS STRIPPED AND BEFORE *THE WORD* THAT LATER SUBJUGATED IT. A VERY IMPORTANT ILLUSTRATION OF THE WAY THAT POETRY IS A CRUCIAL PROPHETIC INSTRUMENT FOR SHATTERING THE SEMANTIC ILLUSIONS THAT CONTROL AND MANIPULATE OUR IMAGINATIONS. WHEN WE CONSIDER THE WORDS OF JESUS IN MATTHEW 20:16, SAYING "SO THE LAST SHALL BE FIRST, AND THE FIRST shall be last.'", we witness its prophetic implications more broadly than the consensus opinion that this was just about a Jewish - Gentile comparison of receptiveness to the good news. The context of Jesus' audience does matter, and it is true that his Jewish audience would have considered themselves "first" in one sense as the offspring of the patriarch Abraham who befriended their God. There is something powerful about Jesus naming and exalting those who have been relegated last to first position, both in his context and beyond. This isn't to deny the dignity of those who believe themselves to be first but is a subversive effort to undermine the very hierarchy of value we impose at the expense of the oppressed.

FURTHER IMPLICATIONS

We can appreciate that framing the worth of existential blackness as pre-existent divinity will be felt by some to be unnecessarily hyperbolic or perhaps blasphemous. But it must be equally acknowledged by those who present that charge that we are up against a ferocious demonization narrative of Blackness that requires an urgent exorcism. A dilemma that we've faced and found prevalent amongst a variety people with religious backgrounds is whether their identity or faith has first priority.   While we appreciate this isn't a straightforward conflict to resolve for many, especially when you take into account that our human identity is multifaceted, and our core

COMMITMENTS SPAN ACROSS MANY DOMAINS.   BUT THE VISION OF BLACKNESS WE'VE TRIED TO PAINT ENCOMPASSES OUR FAITH, OUR PERSONALITY, OUR SEXUALITY INSEPARABLY.   IN OTHER WORDS, PLACING OUR BLACKNESS FIRST WILL NOT ALIENATE ANY ASPECT OF WHO WE ARE, BUT RATHER ENCAPSULATES THEM ALL IN THE SAME COVERING OF

DIGNITY ILLUSTRATED IN GENESIS 1:11-2. OUR BLACKNESS PRECEDES AND ENCOMPASSES ALL OF US.

ATTRIBUTE 2 -

SOVEREIGN

THIS ATTRIBUTE BUILDS ON THE FIRST AND AFFIRMS THAT BLACKNESS CAN DETERMINE ITS OWN SIGNIFICANCE, MEANING AND DESTINY IN VARIED CONTEXTS. IT REQUIRES NO AUTHORIZATION OR VALIDATION FROM WHITENESS TO EXIST. FOR TOO LONG BLACKNESS HAS BEEN SUBSERVIENT, DEEMED

THE OTHER, CLASSED AS INFERIOR OR A MINORITY WHEN NONE OF THESE ARE TRUE IN A GLOBAL EXISTENTIAL WAY.

THIS SOVEREIGNTY PLAYS OUT IN SEVERAL DOMAINS. IT DEMANDS THAT BLACK/ALL BODIES, MINDS AND THEIR SOULS ARE NOT AT THE MERCY OF OTHERS TO DEFINE, DEMONIZE OR PURPOSE. IT DEFIES THE NOTION THAT BLACKNESS IS AN ETHNIC MINORITY TO STEREOTYPE AND PATRONIZE. THE BLACK BODY, INCLUDING THE WAY IT PERFORMS, IT'S SENSE OF AUTONOMY AND SELF-OWNERSHIP, HAS FOR TOO

LONG BEEN OUTSOURCED TO IDEAS OF WHITENESS. IT IS URGENT FOR LIBERATION FOR THE BLACK BODY AND MIND TO RECLAIM THIS SENSE OF SELF-DETERMINATION AND TOTAL AUTONOMY. SOVEREIGNTY OVER THE BLACK BODY SPEAKS POIGNANTLY AGAINST EXPLOITATION OF ITS FUNCTIONS AND PURPOSE BY VARYING METHODS OF FORCED LABOR, SEX TRAFFICKING OR LACK OF PROVISION OF ADEQUATE PUBLIC AND PERSONAL HEALTHCARE. WE THINK SOVEREIGNTY AS IT RELATES TO THE SOUL COULD SPEAK TO A FEW IMPORTANT CONCERNS. THERE IS A GROWING SENSE OF disconnect amongst younger adherents in traditional forms of religion that seem to place a great hold on the souls of Black folk, determining who is saved, by what beliefs or rituals and into what after-life, overriding the individual's agency in the process.   Black sovereignty could give such people the courage to take ownership of their soul, knowing that they exist as part of an ancient

SUBSTANCE THAT PRE-EXISTS ALL FORMS OF RELIGION AND HUMAN PHILOSOPHY.

THE IMPORTANT QUESTION FOR ONE'S OWN BLACK SELF IS WHAT MUST WE DO TO BE SAVED? WHAT HEALING PATHS ARE NEEDED TO BE TAKEN TO ADDRESS THE MALAISES OF OUR MIND, BODY AND SOUL? CAN BLACKNESS BECOME A SACRED GROUND of sufficiency and abundance for all to embrace and find refuge?

ATTRIBUTE 3- CREATIVITY

In the Genesis text, we find the potential to understand Blackness as a mode and means by which things are created and can be reimagined as a co-conspirator and co-creator with whatever one believes is the first cause of all existence. It's important to see

CREATIVITY AS THE FIRST CONSEQUENCE OF BLACKNESS, AS BLACKNESS WAS THE PRECURSOR TO CREATIVITY; THE SACRED PLAYGROUND OF DIVINE CREATIVITY ITSELF. THE CREATIVITY THAT WE WITNESS EXUDING FROM BLACKNESS IS ALSO LIFE GIVING.

WHEN CONSIDERING THE DYNAMIC BREADTH OF CREATIVE EXPRESSION FROM BLACK CULTURE, MANY HAVE FELT A SENSE OF DIVINE AWE, OFTEN DESCRIBED AS "SOULFUL" AND DEEMED VERY DESIRABLE. BLACKNESS HAS UNLIMITED CREATIVE FREEDOM AND

POTENTIAL INTRINSICALLY. WHETHER THIS MANIFESTS IN BLACK MUSICAL, ARTISTIC OR INVENTIVE CREATIVITY. THIS TRUTH MIGHT HELP MORE BLACK PEOPLE WITNESS THIS UNTAPPED POTENTIAL IN THE FACE OF THIS REALIZATION. THE ORIGIN STORY OF BLACKNESS ARTICULATED IN THIS NEO-THEOLOGICAL IMAGINATION PROVIDES A ROBUST CONCEPTUAL BASIS UPON WISH TO AFFIRM THE CREATIVE POTENTIAL OF BLACKNESS. THE DESIRABILITY OF THE CREATIVE POTENTIAL OF BLACKNESS HAS TOO OFTEN BEEN EXPLOITED AT THE EXPENSE OF THE DIGNITY OF THE PEOPLE WHO

EXPRESS IT. SO, THIS REAFFIRMATION OF BLACK CREATIVITY IS FOR THE HEALING OF BLACK CREATIVES WHO FEEL FRUSTRATED AND DISILLUSIONED ABOUT WHO THEY ARE, WHY THEY ARE HERE AND WHAT TO DO WITH THEIR FULL CREATIVE POTENTIAL. PERHAPS THEY SUBMITTED THEIR GIFT TO A RELIGIOUS INSTITUTION THAT RIGIDLY SET THE PARAMETERS AND CONTEXT FOR ITS USAGE AND USED THEIR GIFT WHILE CLAIMING IT'S FOR THE GLORY OF GOD AND NOT ABOUT THEM. THEY WERE MADE CREATIVE SLAVES BEHOLDEN TO A SYSTEM THAT WANTED THEIR PRODUCTIVITY MORE THAN IT WANTED THEM, IT wanted their holiness more than it wanted their wholeness. Then their faith crashed and burned inevitably, upon the penetrating realization that their innate desire to be a creative outlet made them a victim of exploitation.

That's why the total liberation of creativity is found in affirming its underpinning metaphysical value, which defines the reverence and ethics of how we engage creativity. We want to return to the analogy

OF MUSIC BY WHICH TO FURTHER ILLUSTRATE THE POINT.   THE GREATEST POWER OF MUSIC IS THAT INFINITE POTENTIALITY AND UNTETHERED FREEDOM THAT EXISTS TO CHOOSE THE NOTES OF A NOVEL IMPROVISATION.   THAT VASTNESS OF POSSIBILITIES INCLUDES EVERY MUSICAL PATTERN, MELODY, HARMONY, SCALE, RESULTING IN ALL POSSIBLE COLORS - TOGETHER.   THE ONE EXPERIMENT WE CAN EASILY RECALL FROM OUR ART LESSONS AT SCHOOL, IS THAT OF YOU MIX ALL COLOURS TOGETHER, YOU GET BLACK.

ATTRIBUTE 4 –

RESTFULNESS

IN THE BEGINNING GOD CREATED THE HEAVENS AND THE EARTH. THE EARTH WAS FORMLESS AND EMPTY, AND **DARKNESS** *COVERED THE DEEP WATERS. AND THE SPIRIT OF GOD WAS HOVERING OVER THE SURFACE OF THE WATERS.*

THIS PICTURE OF DARKNESS AS A COVERING, RESTING OVER THE UNENDING DEPTHS OF THE FLUID OF LIFE, GIVES US A SENSE OF PEACE IN STILLNESS AND

PROTECTION. WE ALSO SEE HERE THE POTENTIAL INERTIA OF BLACKNESS BEFORE IT BECAME ACTIVATED BY A FORCE OR INTENTION, THIS SPEAKS TO THE INHERENT REST, EFFORTLESS BEING THAT IS INNATE TO BLACKNESS. IT WAS THERE BEFORE IT WAS DISCOVERED. THERE IS NO STRIVING FOR SURVIVAL NECESSARY FOR BLACKNESS IN THAT PRE-EXISTING STATE. BUT BLACKNESS CAN INTERACT WITH AND RESPOND TO CREATIVE MOVEMENT. CREATIVE

Intention and Blackness produce a synergy of endless possibilities.

Rest is a birthright of Blackness, there exists a calm state in which all of the potentiality of Blackness resides and is maximally charged. Rest speaks to the effortlessness of Blackness to exist, that is not in a constant state of survival and striving.   So much Black religion is a historical wrestling with dehumanization, and that is to be expected in light of what happened to the Black body,

MIND AND SOUL. OUR SPIRITS LONG FOR REST FROM THE LABOR OF BLACKNESS IN A WORLD THAT NEVER FEELS LIKE IT WAS BUILT TO BELONG, NOMADS SOJOURNING THROUGH ARID SANDS WHERE THERE IS NO REST FOR THE WICKED OR RIGHTEOUS ALIKE IF YOU HAPPEN TO BE BLACK. REST THEREFORE SEEMS OUT OF REACH AND UNDESERVING IN BLACK CONSCIOUSNESS, THE PURVIEW OF MYTHMAKING AND SKYDREAMING.

BUT IS THERE SUFFICIENT IMAGINATION FOR A PLACE OF REST FROM THIS EXISTENTIAL LABOR? THE VERY sense that existential blackness in the context of our world feels like an exhausting and relentless journey of proving its worth, is a sign of a fall from grace and a need for holistic redemption.

Attribute 5 - Knowability

We see the first inkling of the knowability of blackness in Genesis 1:1-2, as there is some interaction between blackness and another

KNOWABLE ENTITY. BLACKNESS CAN BE RECOGNIZED, ENGAGED, IT CAN CREATE, BIRTH, AND GIVE LIFE TO ALL THINGS. BLACKNESS SEEMS TO REPRESENT THE POTENTIALITY OF ALL THINGS, ALL COLORS, AND THE VERY PLACE FROM WHENCE LIGHT EMERGED. THIS IDEA OF BLACKNESS GIVING BIRTH TO LIGHT USEFULLY CHALLENGES THE COMMONLY HELD NOTION THAT BLACKNESS IS THE ANTITHESIS OF LIGHT.

THIS KNOWABILITY IS KEY BECAUSE IT INCARNATES BLACKNESS AWAY FROM THE REALM OF MERE

OPINION, BELIEF AND SPECULATION, IT BECOMES A SCIENCE, AN EPISTEMOLOGY, AN INTIMATE AWARENESS OF SOMETHING ANCIENT THAT CAN BE WITNESSED. ONE'S BLACKNESS IS KNOWN BY SELF AND QUITE OFTEN OTHER, WITHOUT MUCH NEED FOR COMPREHENSIVE INVESTIGATION OR INTERROGATION. THIS IS OF COURSE IN THE PRIOR SENSE AS LATER PROBLEMS WILL OBFUSCATE THIS SELF-VISIBILITY OF ONE'S BLACKNESS - THIS WILL BE EXPLAINED LATER. THERE IS AN EXCITING AND DEEPLY PROFOUND POTENTIAL TO KNOW ONE'S BLACKNESS FULLY IN A WAY THAT DIFFERS FROM THE potential to know any other aspect of oneself. This knowability speaks to a further consideration as it implies the undeniability of one's Blackness once it has been truly enlightened. For it is impossible for those who were once enlightened, and have tasted the heavenly awareness of one's Blackness, to later reject that enlightenment. It must be urgently stated that this knowability is not in reference to the superficial self-identification of one's Blackness based on trivial tropes and stereotypes in popular culture. We consider those degrees of knowing a display of indoctrinated ignorance disguised as knowledge. Caricatures of blackness crafted by opportunistic culture vultures and those who wish to perpetuate a myopic, insipid and cancerous vision of blackness. The knowability of blackness we refer to here is a kind of epiphany, a gnostic rebirth to the

FORMER GLORY OF BLACKNESS, ACCESSIBLE TO THOSE WHO WILL SEEK IT OUT.

ATTRIBUTE 6 - EXPANSIVE

THE NOTION OF BLACKNESS AS A SOCIOECONOMICALLY LIMITING BURDEN IN THIS LIFE HAS PERHAPS INFECTED THE SOCIETAL IMAGINATION WITH VERY LOW EXPECTATIONS OF BLACKNESS. THE IDEA THAT ONE'S BLACKNESS SHOULD BE SEEN AS LIMITING, SUFFOCATING, AN ENCUMBRANCE TO

EVADE, REMAINS A TOXIC NOOSE TO UNLEASH FROM THE BLACK PSYCHE. POPULAR NOTIONS OF BLACKNESS IN WESTERN SOCIETY ARE OFTEN HEGEMONIC AND HIERARCHICAL, SUBSERVIENT TO THE PHALLUS OF WHITE HETERONORMATIVE PATRIARCHY, GIVING VERY LITTLE ROOM FOR DIVERSE MANIFESTATIONS OF BLACKNESS.

BUT WHEN WE CONSIDER THE ORIGIN STORY WE HAVE OUTLINED ABOVE, THE THING ABOUT BLACKNESS THAT PERHAPS STRIKES US MOST IS JUST HOW ALL-ENCOMPASSING AND EXPANSIVE IT IS AT THE OUTSET.

BLACKNESS THAT BY NECESSITY MANIFESTS IN SO MANY DIFFERENTIATED WAYS, AND DOESN'T INHERENTLY PRIORITIZE ONE MANIFESTATION OVER ANOTHER IN THE WAY SOCIETY HAS MADE THE UNFORTUNATE HABIT OF. A MODEL OF EXISTENTIAL BLACKNESS SEEMS TO EMERGE IN OUR MIND THAT CRITIQUES OTHER FORMS OF BLACKNESS THAT ARE LESS ACCOMMODATING OF DIVERSITY. BLACKNESS OF VARYING SHADES, SHAPES, FORGED INTO DIFFERENTLY MANIFESTED WAYS OF BEING, LOVING AND LIVING. A KIND OF BLACKNESS THAT WE CAN ALL FIND EXPANDING DEGREES OF EXISTENTIAL

LIBERTY, WHERE WE NEED NOT YEARN FOR VALIDATION BECAUSE IT IS FOUND ENTIRELY IN THIS COMMUNAL, EXISTENTIAL BLACKNESS.

ATTRIBUTE 7 - BEAUTY

"BLACK IS BEAUTIFUL" IS NOT SIMPLY A CASUAL REMARK BUT A HEALING DECLARATION WITH POWERFUL PROPHETIC IMPLICATIONS. PART OF WHAT WE HOPE TO OUTLINE IN THE FOLLOWING CHAPTERS IS HOW THIS ATTRIBUTE WAS MARRED,

HOW WE CONTINUE TO SINFULLY PERPETUATE THE HARM THAT WAS CAUSED AND HOW WE MUST COUNTER THIS WITH THE GOSPEL OF BLACK'S BEAUTY. THE BEAUTY WE ARE ATTEMPTING TO EXPLICATE IS NOT MERELY THE SUBJECTIVE AND SUPERFICIAL, BUT AN ABIDING COMFORT AND CONFIDENCE WITH ONE'S PRESENCE AND SIGNIFICANCE IN THE WORLD.

BLACK IS BEAUTIFUL.

SO, WHAT WE HAVE SO FAR OUTLINED IS THE ONTOLOGICAL REALITY OF BLACKNESS AS

SOMETHING THAT IS PRE-EXISTENT DIVINITY, SOVEREIGN, KNOWABLE, CREATIVE, RESTFUL, EXPANSIVE, BEAUTIFUL. WE CAN CONSIDER THESE THE FORMATIVE ATTRIBUTES OF BLACKNESS.

THE TRINITY OF BLACKNESS - BLACKBODY, BLACKMIND, BLACKSOUL.

BLACKOLOGY AS AN ONTOLOGY OF BLACKNESS:

FOR BLACKNESS TO BE CONSIDERED SOMETHING TO BE OR BECOME, WE ARE FORCED TO CONTEMPLATE THE DIFFERENT MODES AND MECHANISMS OF BEING IN THIS WORLD. PRAGMATICALLY SPEAKING, WE CAN DEFINE ONTOLOGICAL REALITY AS EITHER PHYSICAL OR

METAPHYSICAL. THE PHYSICALITY OF BEING SPEAKS TO A KIND OF TANGIBILITY THAT CAN BE PERCEIVED BEYOND MERE ABSTRACTION AND DOESN'T REQUIRE DEBATE TO AFFIRM OR ESTABLISH. THERE IS A SENSE IN WHICH BLACKNESS IS THE TANGIBILITY OF ALL THINGS. WHAT DOES THAT MEAN? WELL AT THE SUBATOMIC LEVEL AND EVEN WHEN CONSIDERING THINGS AT THE MACRO LEVEL, THERE IS MORE SPACE THAN THERE IS MATTER. IT IS THE VERY SPACE OF BLACKNESS THAT DEFINES AND ARRANGES WHAT IS POSSIBLE TO TANGIBLY EXIST. EVEN OUR PERCEPTION OF COLOR IS DEFINED BY VARYING DEGREES AND SHADES OF

BLACKNESS. SO, WE CAN START BY IDENTIFYING THE FIRST MANIFESTATION OF BLACKNESS AS PHYSICAL EMBODIMENT. IT MUST BE SAID AT THE OUTSET THAT A HOLISTIC VIEW OF BLACKNESS MUST INCORPORATE ITS METAPHYSICAL DIMENSIONS. IT'S FOR THIS REASON WE FIND IT USEFUL TO USE THE METAPHOR OF HUMAN EMBODIMENT TO ARTICULATE THE MULTIDIMENSIONAL NATURE OF BLACKNESS. WE OFTEN REFER TO THE BODY, MIND AND SOUL OF THE HUMAN BODY AS ITS COMPOSITE PARTS, WITH THE BODY REPRESENTING ITS TANGIBLE PHYSICALITY AND

THE MIND/SOUL REPRESENTING THE METAPHYSICAL ASPECTS.

THE TRINITY OF BLACKNESS

"IT IS RELATIONSHIP THAT PROVIDES THE BACKDROP AND FRAMING FOR THE ART OF OUR LIVES, APART FROM WHICH OUR COLORS WOULD SIMPLY DISPERSE INTO THE DARKNESS FORMLESS AND VOID, AWAITING THE HOVERING OF THE SPIRIT TO COLLECT THEM AND—WITH her shades and hues—breathe into us to set them free"

— Richard Rohr

We postulate that Blackness, the divine essence of all isness, manifests in human locality as three subcategories; namely: Blackbody, Blackmind and Blacksoul.

These triune subcategories are unique expressions of one essence, co-equal in divine value and priority. They each provide a particular vantage point by which to interpret and critique Black lived experiences, and will be the modalities by which we articulate Blackology.

These categories aren't novel, comprehensive or exclusive to any other aspect of Blackness at the physical or metaphysical level, but they provide a definitive framework to conceptualize the challenges, threats, solutions and hopes of Blackness in a holistic, integrative manner. This explicit use of the

CHRISTIAN TERM TRINITY SPEAKS TO THE NOTION THAT EACH CATEGORY IS SUFFICIENTLY DISTINCT, NEEDING ACKNOWLEDGEMENT OF ITS PARTICULAR FUNCTION AND FOCUS, YET ARE CO-EQUAL IN IMPORTANCE AND CO-SUBSTANTIVE IN DEFINING BLACKNESS.

DEFINITIONS:

BLACKBODY

THE BLACKBODY IS THE PHYSICAL BLACK CORPUS, WHATEVER ITS SHAPE, SHADE OF MELANIN, SEX, GENDER, ABILITY, AND VARIED PHYSIOLOGICAL, TACTILE AND SAFETY NEEDS. THIS SPEAKS TO THE INDIVIDUAL BLACK BODY AND THE WAY IT IS COLLECTIVELY PERCEIVED, IMAGINED AND TREATED THROUGH THE LENS OF SOCIETAL AESTHETICS, POLITICS AND RELIGION.

THE BLACKBODY INTERPENETRATES INSEPARABLY WITH BLACKMIND AND BLACKSOUL, BUT IS THE MOST TACTILE EXPRESSION OF BLACK EMBODIMENT.

BLACKMIND

THIS BLACKMIND REFERS TO THE PSYCHOLOGICAL DOMAIN INCLUDING BLACK THOUGHT AND BLACK INTELLIGENCE; HOW THIS MANIFESTS THROUGH TIME IN ITS VARIED WAYS, NUANCED BY CULTURE, EXPERIENCE AND EDUCATION. IT SPEAKS TO ITS STRENGTHS AND VULNERABILITIES, ITS POTENTIALITY AND SCOPE OF IMPACT ON THE BLACKBODY AND BLACKSOUL.

BLACKSOUL

BLACKSOUL IS THE SEAT OF DESIRE, EMOTION, CREATIVITY AND SPIRIT. BLACKSOUL AND BLACKMIND ARE IN MANY REGARDS INTERCHANGEABLE AND EQUALLY INTANGIBLE, BUT SOUL GIVES SPACES TO THE MYSTERIOUS AND INEFFABLE ASPECTS OF BLACKNESS. IT CONJURES UP THE MYSTERY AND THE MAGIC WITHIN BLACKNESS, THAT MOST CERTAINLY FINDS EXPRESSION ITSELF IN ALL 3 ELEMENTS.

We hope it serves to illustrate vividly and with strong language some of the existential angst and rage that arises in the process of navigating life in the body, mind and soul of dystopian Blackness.

There are a few themes in the passage that we want to explicate the existential trajectory of Black embodiment in the lattice of racialized oppression.

Blackbody, Blackmind and Blacksoul in the above passage is painted, and revealed in many modalities, in a scene of torment and despair. It seems starved of affection and attention, feeling unwanted, embittered and despised. How did it arrive in this precipice of despair? What were the murky roads to perdition?

A critical examination of the pathology of the Blackbody, Blackmind and Blacksoul through the distorted lens of whiteness:

THIS POSITION OF THE BLACKBODY AS EXPENDABLE HAS MADE IT SYNONYMOUS WITH DEATH, DESERVING OF DEATH, AND DEATH OF THE BLACKBODY IS NO LONGER LAMENTABLE TO OUR COLLECTIVE MORAL CONSCIENCE, BUT INEVITABLE - NECESSARY BY NATURAL DESIGN. THIS CAN BE SEEN PLAYED OUT IN THE WAY THE BLACKBODY IS TREATED IN WHITE MAJORITY SOCIETIES, WHERE ITS PRESENCE IN CERTAIN NEIGHBORHOODS IS AUTOMATICALLY SEEN AS AN INFESTATION TO EXTERMINATE USING THE POLICE. WE CAN RECALL SEEING VIDEO FOOTAGE OF THE LIFELESS BODY OF GEORGE FLOYD LAYING IN THE street unattended and disregarded after taking an officer's knee to the neck for 8 minutes and 46 seconds as if his blackbody was utterly meaningless. There was a sense in which this was to be seen as the norm as this was mostly typical and yet not at the same time. George Floyd's body was wounded, crushed and asphyxiated for the world to see on camera. That finally got the world's attention for about a month or two.

THE BLACKBODY HAS ALSO HISTORICALLY BEEN DEEMED THE ANTITHESIS OF BEAUTY, THE EPICENTER OF DISGUST BY THE WHITE EMBODIED GAZE. STRANGE FRUIT BY ... ENCAPSULATED THIS POETICALLY IN THE REFERENCE, "THE BULGIN' EYES AND THE TWISTED MOUTH."

CONSIDER THIS PROPHETIC REIMAGINING OF SCRIPTURE TO GIVE THEOLOGICAL LANGUAGE TO THE SOCIAL AESTHETICS OF BLACKNESS THROUGH THE DISTORTIONS OF WHITENESS:

THE BLACKBODY HAD NO BEAUTY OR MAJESTY TO ATTRACT US TO IT, NOTHING IN ITS APPEARANCE THAT WE SHOULD DESIRE IT. IT WAS DESPISED AND REJECTED BY MANKIND, A VESSEL OF SUFFERING, AND FAMILIAR WITH PAIN. LIKE ONE FROM WHOM PEOPLE HIDE THEIR FACES, DESPISED, AND WE HELD IT IN LOW ESTEEM.

INSPIRED BY ISAIAH 53.

THIS PRESUMED UGLINESS OF THE BLACKBODY HAS BEEN DEEPLY INGRAINED IN OUR SOCIETAL

CONSCIOUSNESS, AND INCORPORATES HOW FACIAL FEATURES, HAIR TEXTURE AND BODY DIMENSIONS OF THE BLACKBODY ARE PERCEIVED. THE TRAGEDY OF THIS IS HOW EVEN YOUNG CHILDREN ALREADY BEGIN TO BELIEVE THESE IDEAS ABOUT THE INFERIORITY AND SUSPICIOUSNESS OF THE BLACKBODY, LONG BEFORE WE WOULD IMAGINE THIS TO BE THE CASE. THIS MEANS THAT THE TOXIC IDEAS OF THE BLACKBODY ARE OFTEN ALREADY ENTRENCHED SIGNIFICANTLY BEFORE THE TEENAGE YEARS WHERE MANY YOUTHS ARE GRAPPLING WITH SELF-ESTEEM ISSUES.

This contempt in the open towards the blackbody is paradoxically coupled with a clandestine white fetishization of its sexual prowess, that is exploitative and violent. The blackbody is often seen as something to be bought or stolen as a plaything for pleasure, rather than something to love, treasure and honor. More could be said about the sexualization of the blackbody to fill an entire book, but it's worth acknowledging here that the cis-heteronormative lens of society means queer and genderqueer bodies are considered even more perverse and unworthy of dignity or liberation. The intersection of gender, sexuality and class creates layers of disadvantage that nuances how the blackbody experiences this prejudice. The blackbody is rarely bestowed dignity by default and often how dominant society imagines and depicts the devilish, but rarely the divine. The blackbody is often deemed subservient, theologized as slave and to be trod upon without repair or remorse. To be slapped, choked, raped and shot, with

IMPUNITY. WHAT IS THE COST OF THIS TRAUMATIC PARADIGM ON THE BLACKBODY?

STRANGE FRUIT

SOUTHERN TREES BEAR A STRANGE FRUIT

BLOOD ON THE LEAVES AND BLOOD AT THE ROOT

BLACK BODIES SWINGIN' IN THE SOUTHERN BREEZE

STRANGE FRUIT HANGIN' FROM THE POPLAR TREES

PASTORAL SCENE OF THE GALLANT SOUTH

THE BULGIN' EYES AND THE TWISTED MOUTH

SCENT OF MAGNOLIAS SWEET AND FRESH

THEN THE SUDDEN SMELL OF BURNIN' FLESH

HERE IS A FRUIT FOR THE CROWS TO PLUCK

FOR THE RAIN TO GATHER

FOR THE WIND TO SUCK

FOR THE SUN TO ROT

FOR THE TREE TO DROP

HERE IS A STRANGE AND BITTER CROP

SONGWRITER: LEWIS ALLAN

THE BLACKMIND IS TOO OFTEN DEEMED UNWORTHY

OF EDUCATION UNLESS IT'S THE RELIGIOUS KIND.   THIS

IS INTENTIONAL AS A MEANS TO MENTAL INCARCERATION. THE BLACKMIND HAS BEEN INDOCTRINATED INTO A CONCRETE SENSE OF INFERIORITY, ENNOBLED SELF-DENIAL, ACCEPTING IT'S SUFFERING AND THAT OF THE BLACKBODY AS DIVINE MANDATE.

THE IDENTITY OF VIOLENCE THAT HAS BEEN PERPETUATED BY CONCEPTUALIZING GOD AS WHITE, I.E. THE DEIFICATION OF WHITENESS, HAS LEFT MANY PSYCHOLOGICAL SCARS IN THE BLACK IMAGINATION AND BLACK SELF-ASPIRATION. IT HAS LEFT MANY

BLACKSOULS LONGING TO "BE MADE AS WHITE AS SNOW" FOR THEIR SANCTIFICATION.

THE BLACKMIND IS THE GATEWAY TO THE BLACK IMAGINATION, AND IS THE MEANS BY WHICH SELF-PERCEPTIONS OF BLACKNESS CAN BE INFLUENCED FOR GOOD OR EVIL.

IF WE REVERT TO THE ORIGINAL PASSAGE FOR REFLECTION, THE BLACKMIND UNDER THE STRAIN OF THESE WORLDLY PRESSURES IS SUBDUED, DEPRESSED AND CONFORMED TO THE PATTERN OF THIS WORLD.

NOTICE THE PATHOLOGY OF THIS DISEASE PERMEATES AT EVERY LEVEL, WHICH LEADS ME TO DESCRIBE THE IMPACT ON BLACKSOUL.

THE BLACKSOUL REMAINS THE DYNAMIC FOUNTAIN OF THE MYSTIQUE AND MAGIC OF BLACKNESS IN SPITE OF THE TOXICITIES THAT HAVE PLAGUED BLACKBODY, AND BLACKMIND WITH THE INTENT ON POISONING THE BLACKSOUL. IT HAS HOWEVER BECOME FAMILIAR WITH GRIEF AND DESPAIR, OFTEN SATURATING IT'S CREATIVE POTENTIAL AND CAPACITY TOWARDS LAMENTING THE CURRENT STATE OF THINGS. WE

Consider the melancholy nature of black spiritual music, that articulates sorrow about the world and longing for the respite of Beulah Land, and we can't help but wonder about the existential price tag of this burden. This particular excerpt resonated as it describes the self-destructive nature of the malady of the blacksoul we sometimes perpetuate:

"We are also often virulent conduits of our own despising; we encapsulate the

PROGRAMMED CONTEMPT OF OUR BLACKBODIES, CULTURE, AND SPIRITUALITY LIKE THE MAD COW DISEASE THAT SLOWLY ERODES THE BRAINS OF ITS UNSUSPECTING VICTIMS."

HOW DOES ONE CONTEND FOR BLACKNESS IN A WORLD WHERE ANTI-BLACKNESS IS SO INGRAINED AND WEDDED TO ETHICS OF WESTERN PHILOSOPHY AND SOCIAL PRIORITIES?

SO WHAT WENT WRONG? - THE FRACTURING OF BLACKNESS THROUGH THE SINFUL PREDILECTIONS OF WHITE SUPREMACY.

THE ORIGINAL SIN THAT ENTERED THE GARDEN WAS THE IDEA THAT BEARING THE DIVINE IMAGE OF BLACKNESS WAS A CURSE, SUBSEQUENTLY ERRONEOUSLY DEEMED THE CURSE OF HAM BY ABRAHAMIC RELIGION. THE ORIGINAL SIN OF BLACK SELF-DOUBT, SELF-DEPRECIATION IS A DELUSION OF GRANDEUR INHERITED THROUGH PERPETUATING THE LIE THAT WHITENESS IS THE GLORIFICATION OF MAN.

BLACKNESS BECAME PERSONIFIED AS EVIL, AND THERE WAS A HISTORIC WHITENING OF GOD - THE DEIFICATION OF WHITENESS WHICH WAS THE HIGHEST SEAL OF WHITE SUPREMACY.

ONE OF THE WAYS RACISM WORKS IS THAT IT MAKES BLACK PEOPLE BELIEVE THE MOST NOBLE, LEGITIMATE AND URGENT MISSION IS TO CIVILIZE OURSELVES INSTEAD OF LIBERATING OURSELVES. HISTORICALLY, THIS IS BECAUSE WE HAVE CURATED A MUSEUM OF LIES ABOUT BLACKNESS AND FORCE FED POISONOUS IDEAS about our inherent inferiority as the real reason for our predicament in this world.

That's where the impact of racism needs radical healing intervention too as liberation is our only hope.

The liberation of the Black Trinity demands an intentional disavowal of its conditioned perception of whiteness as supremely divine. Only once whiteness is dethroned, and blackness is sanitized of its stigma, will the

BLACKMIND, BLACKBODY AND BLACKSOUL BE RESTORED TO ITS ORIGINAL STATE OF WHOLENESS AS THE CENTRAL MANIFESTATION OF THE IMAGO DEI.

BLACK TRINITY DIALOGUE -

JEFF HOOD:

IN CONSIDERING THE INCARNATION OF THESE THINGS IN ONE'S LIVED EXPERIENCE, I AM REMINDED OF THE LEGACIES OF YOUR HOMELAND JAMAICA. IN A LOT OF WAYS, WHEN I THINK OF THE PERFECTION OF THE BLACKBODY, THE BLACKMIND AND THE BLACKSOUL, FOR WHATEVER REASON, BOB MARLEY COMES TO MIND. WHEN I THINK ABOUT THE BLACK BODY, AND I THINK ABOUT THE INCARNATION OF THE BLACK body, I'm not just thinking about the way that the body looks or the way that the body is shaped or all of these aesthetics, it's almost like the comfort, one's comfort in their own body — I think that Marley seemed to have had that comfort in his own being. That was important. And I think along the lines of the Blackmind, Marley is living in a way and mentality that is different, that pushes back against colonialism while simultaneously interacting with colonialism in a way that protests, but also seeks to unearth human

CONNECTION WITH THE COLONIZER AS WELL. AND AS FAR AS THE BLACKSOUL IS CONCERNED, I THINK ABOUT MARLEY'S SONG "COULD YOU BE LOVED", AND HOW THE INCARNATION OF THE BLACKSOUL— THE FULLNESS OF THE BLACKSOUL IS THIS LOVE OF THE BLACKBODY, LOVE OF COMMUNITY, LOVE OF WORLD. I REALLY FEEL LIKE MIND, BODY AND SOUL REALLY FOUND MUCH EXPRESSION IN THE MUSIC OF MARLEY AND PERHAPS EVEN IN OTHER CHANNELS OF HIS CREATIVE EXPRESSION BEYOND THAT. MUSIC IN GENERAL IS QUITE REPRESENTATIVE OF THE INCARNATION OF BLACKNESS, OF BLACKOLOGY

MANIFESTING AS THE BLACKMIND, THE BLACKBODY AND THE BLACKSOUL.

YOEL OMOWALE:

YEAH, WE THINK IT'S GREAT THAT YOU BROUGHT UP BOB MARLEY BECAUSE HE IS SOMEONE WHOSE LEGACY IS INSEPARABLY CLOSE TO MY HEART, I DO REMEMBER IN CHILDHOOD, VISITING TRENCHTOWN, KINGSTON WHERE HE GREW UP LIKE ROSE IN A CONCRETE GARDEN. IT REALLY WAS A PRECIPICE OF DESPAIR AND SCARCITY WHERE THE BLACKBODY WAS

CHARGRILLED IN THE FEROCIOUS BLAZE OF POVERTY. TRENCHTOWN PROMISED NO ONE WHEN AND WHERE THEIR NEXT MEAL MIGHT ARRIVE. THE BLACKMIND WAS AGAIN, OPPRESSED THROUGH AN INTENTIONAL DEPRIVATION OF EDUCATION AND COLONIAL MANIFESTATIONS OF OPPRESSIVE RELIGION CREATED A LOT OF SPIRITUAL VIOLENCE THAT A CONSCIOUS BLACKSOUL LIKE MARLEY'S HAD TO ESCAPE. YET YOU FIND MARLEY EMERGES FROM THAT ABYSS, AND USES HIS PSALMS OF DELIVERANCE TO RISE FROM THE ASHES AND LEAD A REVOLUTION IN HUMAN SOLIDARITY. SOMEHOW HIS BLACKSOUL SURVIVED AND THRIVED

DESPITE THE FACT THAT IT WAS NOT MEANT TO, NO ONE SHOULD SURVIVE WITHIN THAT KIND OF ENVIRONMENT AND NOT BE TAINTED AND HIS BLACKSOULS SONG WAS A SOURCE OF HIS OWN LIBERATION. HE USED THOSE DEVICES OF HIS SOUL TO CHANNEL THE SUPPORT OF HIS ANCESTORS TO EMPOWER HIMSELF TO A PLACE WHERE HE COULD FIND LOVE FOR HIS OWN BODY, A GIFT THAT GAVE HIM FREEDOM WAS HIS INNER WITNESS OF A BLACK MESSIAH.

JEFF HOOD:

RIGHT, RIGHT. RIGHT. I THINK IT'S IMPORTANT TO FIND OURSELVES BACK IN JAMAICA. AND IT'S INTERESTING HOW AS A SOCIOPOLITICAL SPACE, JAMAICA, IN AND OF ITSELF, REPRESENTS COLLECTIVELY THIS TRINITY OF BLACKNESS. AND WHAT I MEAN BY THAT IS, YOU HAVE THIS SOCIETY THAT IS STRUGGLING TO DECIDE WHETHER OR NOT THEY WANT TO BE A PART OF THE COMMONWEALTH, THEY'RE DECIDING WHO THEY WANT TO BE AND WHAT IT LOOKS LIKE TO BE AN INDEPENDENT REPUBLIC, THEY'RE DECIDING HOW THEY WANT TO INTERACT with capitalism. They're deciding what it looks like to maintain the blackbody, blackmind and the blacksoul in the midst of modernity. And so while Marley is certainly a microcosm of that, I think you also see that in the wake of a lot of black societies; in the wake of colonialism as a whole.

YOEL OMOWALE:

Yeah, I strongly agree with that. And I think Marley clearly represents a wider Rastafarian movement that we must acknowledge, as we talk about him. Rastafari really provided the theological, political and linguistic tools to intelligently critique the systems of power that were at work, the principalities that incarcerated and suffocated so much life. These forces were creating so much disruption and destruction, and poisoning the blackmind, the blackbody, and the blacksoul. Even in my own spiritual journey, my primary introduction to Rastafarianism as an impressionable, traditional Christian boy, was seeing it as a dark and corrupting force for evil. The popular narrative was that Rastafarianism was a trick of the enemy that Christians should unite against. And it wasn't until my later years in life, after really grappling my own sense of identity and having what many might call a crisis of religious faith, we found such existential clarity in examining the cultural, social and spiritual footprints of Rastafari through Bob Marley's legacy and many other demonized Black prophets.

JEFF HOOD:

RIGHT, RIGHT. RIGHT. YEAH. YOU KNOW, IT'S BLACK MOVEMENTS LIKE RASTAFARI AND EVEN OTHER MANIFESTATIONS OF CHRISTIANITY, IN AFRICA AND OTHER SPACES, THAT WE SEE THAT RELIGION, IN AND OF ITSELF IS OFTEN USED AS A VEHICLE TO LIBERATE THE BLACKBODY, THE BLACKMIND AND THE BLACKSOUL. BUT I THINK ONE OF THE THINGS THAT PERHAPS IS BEYOND ORGANIZED RELIGION, OR EVEN AN INSTITUTIONAL RELIGION, OR THE PEOPLE LIKE

Marley and others, the people who somehow are able, in the midst of all of the oppression, in the midst of all of the negativity, under the thumb of the downpressors, who were able to step out and say, I have found this Trinity! I am this Trinity! And I think that that speaks to the Christ event. When I look at the life of James Baldwin, I see someone who is comfortable in his own skin, I look at someone whose mind is developed not by the entrapments of the prevailing culture, but by the wisdom of the ancestors. We are looking straight into the

BLACKSOUL, THE EXPLOSIVE POWER WITH WHICH BALDWIN MOVES THROUGHOUT THE WORLD IS UNDENIABLE.   AND WE SEE THE SAME ESSENCE IN MALCOLM X AS WE DO IN ARETHA FRANKLIN.   I MENTIONED A LOT OF THESE DIFFERENT NAMES BECAUSE I DO FEEL LIKE THERE ARE THESE CHRIST EVENTS WHERE IT SEEMS LIKE THERE IS A COMPLETE INCARNATION OF THE BLACK TRINITY.   THERE IS A COMPLETE INCARNATION OF THE BLACKBODY, THE BLACKMIND AND THE BLACKSOUL.   AND WHEN IT HAPPENS, IT IS INCREDIBLY SPECIAL...BECAUSE IT DOESN'T HAPPEN ENOUGH.

YOEL OMOWALE:

YEAH, WHAT COMES TO MIND IS THAT THE THEOLOGICAL TERM, EPIPHANY OR EVEN MORE SPECIFICALLY A CHRISTOPHANY. THIS IDEA OF CHRIST'S EMBODIED MANIFESTATION IN DIFFERENT LOCATIONS THROUGHOUT TIME. FOR INSTANCE, WITH THE RASTAFARI THEOLOGY OF WHICH I'M CERTAINLY NO EXPERT, BUT IN MY RUDIMENTARY UNDERSTANDING I BELIEVE THAT HAILE SELASSIE WAS, UNDERSTOOD TO BE A MANIFESTATION OF A CHRIST IN

A METAPHYSICAL SENSE, OR SOME KIND OF FULFILMENT PROPHETICALLY TO USHER A PEOPLE TO AWAKEN FROM THE SPELL OF COLONIALISM AND TO LOOK TO AFRICA FOR THEIR REDEMPTION. ONE OF THE THINGS THAT COMES TO MIND WHEN YOU MENTIONED THESE NAMES, LIKE JAMES BALDWIN, MARLEY AND ARETHA, WE SEE BLACKBODIES, WITH THEIR BLACKMINDS WITH THEIR BLACKSOULS, OFTENTIMES IN THESE EXTREMELY HARSH CONDITIONS, AND SUFFERING. THEN THERE IS THIS MOMENT WHERE THE LIGHT COMES ON, AND THEY BECOME A WITNESS, THEY'RE NOT JUST ABLE TO SEE THEIR OWN SUFFERING,

THEY'RE ABLE TO WITNESS THE PLIGHT OF PEOPLE AND OFTENTIMES THE PLIGHT OF PEOPLE EVEN BEYOND THOSE THAT LOOK LIKE THEM.   THEY'RE ABLE TO RECOGNIZE THE SUFFERING OF WOMEN, OF QUEER PEOPLE OR PEOPLE OF OTHER RACES, WHO ARE STRUGGLING IN SOME SYSTEM, AND REMAINING FAITHFUL TO HONOR THAT INNER WITNESS THAT KNOWS- WRONG IS WRONG, REGARDLESS OF WHO'S IN POWER AND WHO HAS THE MONEY.   WE HAVE TO SPEAK OUT AND WE HAVE TO USE EVERY DEVICE TO RESIST.   SOMETHING INSIDE BUBBLES UP LIKE A STIRRING OF THE BLACKSOUL.   I THINK OF AN enslaved Black persons that felt that divine anger about their unjust predicament so they sang a song.   Many of those songs have become spirituals sung in many Black churches.   They resonate with the same soul stirring power as they did hundreds of years ago….because they are melodies from heaven. There is that moment, often creativity plays a part on birthing, that this inner witness says, enough is enough.   Something rises up, and the Black Trinity really resurrects life in that moment.

JEFF HOOD:

RIGHT, I WAS THINKING, AS WE DRAW THIS BRIEF DIALOGUE TO A CLOSE, THAT THE BLACKBODY, THE BLACKMIND, AND THE BLACKSOUL ARE ALWAYS PROPHETIC, BECAUSE BLACK IS ALWAYS GOING TO STAND OUT IN A SEA OF WHITE.   BLACK IS ALWAYS GOING TO PUSH BACK AGAINST THIS COLONIZATION OF THE WORLD, IT'S ALWAYS GOING TO PUSH BACK AGAINST BLENDING IN.   AND SO BLACK IS NOT JUST ABOUT MELANIN, A SKIN COLOR, IT'S ALSO ABOUT A

STATE OF BEING...A WAY OF BEING...A WAY OF KNOWING. AND SO I GUESS I'M ALSO TRYING TO SAY THAT AS WE TOUCH, AS WE ENGAGE, AS WE MOVE AND AS WE THINK ABOUT THIS BLACKBODY, BLACKMIND AND BLACKSOUL, WE ARE GOING TO THIS SPACE OF THE PROPHETIC. AND THAT TO HAVE THE BLACKBODY IS PROPHETIC, TO BE WHO YOU ARE IN YOUR OWN BODY IS PROPHETIC. TO HAVE THE BLACKMIND IS PROPHETIC TO THINK DIFFERENTLY, IS PROPHETIC. TO HAVE THE BLACKSOUL IS PROPHETIC. IT FEELS, LOOKS AND IS EXPERIENCED DIFFERENTLY BEING YOUR OWN AUTHENTIC SELF AND BEING

COMFORTABLE IN YOUR OWN SKIN. ALONG WITH THAT, BLACKNESS IS ALWAYS IS GOING TO EXIST TO PUSH BACK AGAINST, TO RESIST THE, THE BLANDNESS OR THE ERASING NATURE OF WHITENESS, THAT BLACKNESS, THIS BLACKBODY, BLACKMIND, BLACKSOUL, IS ALWAYS GOING TO EXIST TO PROPHETICALLY PUSH BACK...BECAUSE GOD...THE SOURCE OF RIGHTEOUSNESS...IS BLACK. AND IF WE ARE GOING TO EMBODY THE FULLNESS OF THE DIVINE, THEN WE TOO HAVE TO LEARN HOW TO BE BLACK, HOW TO PUSH BACK, HOW TO HAVE A MIND THAT IS ABLE TO SUSTAIN ITSELF THAT DOESN'T NEED ANYBODY

ELSE...A SOUL THAT IS ABLE TO SUSTAIN ITSELF AND NOT NEED ANYBODY ELSE...A BODY THAT DOESN'T NEED ANYONE ELSE THAT CAN MOVE THROUGHOUT THE WORLD AND ENGAGE WITH THE WORLD IN WAYS OF LOVE...BUT NOT HAVING TO BE TOLD HOW TO MOVE. AND I THINK THAT THAT'S THE BEAUTY OF THIS PROJECT AND THAT'S THE BEAUTY OF BLACKOLOGY.

170

THE BLACK PENTECOST

BY RECORD OF THE NEW TESTAMENT AND THE TESTIMONY OF BELIEVER'S IN ANTIQUITY, THE INDWELLING, OUTWARDLY MANIFESTING HOLY SPIRIT; WAS AND IS CAPABLE OF PERFORMING NATURE-BENDING MIRACLES ON REQUEST. THIS WAS INTENDED TO MAKING THE BELIEVER RIGHTEOUS...BUT

OUR CONTENTION IS THAT THE BLACK PENTECOST IS WHAT MAKES US WHOLE.

JEFF HOOD:

SO, IT SEEMS TO ME THAT WHAT IS GOING ON IN THE WORLD...WHAT BLACKNESS IS DOING IN THE WORLD...IS THAT BLACKNESS IS CONSTANTLY BRINGING OUT THE FLAVOR IN THE WORLD. IT'S CONSTANTLY DRAWING US BACK TO SPACES OF EXCITEMENT...SPACES THAT ALLOW US TO BE DIFFERENT IN ORDER TO MAKE A DIFFERENCE...A TRUE

FULLNESS OF LIFE. DURING PENTECOST, THE SPIRIT OF GOD COMES DOWN AND PEOPLE ARE SPEAKING ALL DIFFERENT KINDS OF LANGUAGES AND DOING ALL DIFFERENT KINDS OF THINGS...AND SO IT IS WITH BLACKNESS. BLACKNESS HAS TOUCHED THE ENTIRE WORLD...IT IS A SPIRIT GOING THROUGHOUT ALL THE WORLD...AND WE'RE WITNESSING THE MIRACULOUS. WE'RE HEARING THE SPIRIT OF GOD, MOVE AND SHAPE AND GO, INHALE, EXHALE, DO ALL THESE DIFFERENT THINGS. AND IT SHOWS JUST HOW IF WE ARE WILLING TO EMBRACE BLACKNESS, HOW MUCH OUR LIVES CAN CHANGE. I MEAN, YOU KNOW, JESUS SAYS, "IN THOSE days, as you embrace the message, as you embrace Blackness, you will see greater things than these." And so I feel like Blackness is constantly showing us these greater things. These more exciting things...these more flavorful...these more divine things.

YOEL OMOWALE:

I think that's a really interesting way of interpreting the meaning of Pentecost. It takes us outside of just a traditional rendering of that story, extrapolating a broader meaning of the passage through the lenses of blackology. Part of the tragedy is that Pentecost has often been reduced to a religious event in certain Christian circles, where it's exclusively reserved for a small subset of initiated believers called Pentecostals. It's a bit of a shake, shuffle and shando, a hyper-emotional experience thought to be empowering for ministry. But what if there was something so much more magical, so much more expansive and inclusive, that it was

INVITING HUMANITY, TO TASTE AND SEE. WHAT YOU DESCRIBE SOUNDS LIKE AN EXPANSIVE, BEAUTIFUL AWAKENING, THAT BEGAN LIKE A PENTECOST EVENT, AN OUTPOURING RESTORATION OF BLACKNESS AND IN ITS FULLEST EXTENT, THAT WE ARE INVITED TO BE BAPTIZED IN. SO AS YOU SAID, WE ARE TO EMBRACE THE DIVERSITY, EMBRACE THE POWER OF THE CREATIVITY, THAT IT REKINDLES AND INVITES US TO ENCOUNTER AFRESH AGAIN AND AGAIN.

JEFF HOOD:

Right, you know, I was thinking, you know, what you see at Pentecost is human beings made fully alive...as they are taken from the space of the mundane into vibrant life. That they might have life and have it more abundantly!

You know, the Spirit comes that we might have life and have an abundance: this Spirit of Blackness takes this white space, takes this blank canvas, and creates life. It gives meaning to the canvas, it gives meaning to life. Blackness is a fuel almost that ignites life. And

SO, I THINK IT'S IMPORTANT TO TALK ABOUT THE ACCOMPLISHMENTS AND THE AMAZING NATURE OF BLACK PEOPLE, BUT WHEN THIS NOTION OF BLACKOLOGY, THE SPIRIT OF BLACKNESS, WHEN IT GETS A HOLD OF US, WE ALL BECOME FULLY ALIVE. IT ADDS DEFINITION, IT ADDS COLOR, IT ADDS PERSPECTIVE, IN A WAY THAT WHITENESS NEVER COULD OR EVER WILL.

YOEL OMOWALE:

I THINK, AGAIN, I GUESS THE IMAGE THAT COMES TO MIND, IS AT THE POINT PRIOR TO PENTECOST, YOU HAVE THIS GROUP OF FAITHFUL DISCIPLES WHO ARE STILL TRYING TO FIGURE OUT WHAT THEY'RE GOING TO DO. AND THEN AS YOU SAID, THERE IS THIS EXPLOSION OF POWER THAT ARRIVES AND CHANGES EVERYTHING. AND I THINK THAT WHAT YOU'RE INVITING US TO CONSIDER AND I THINK MAKES SENSE TO ME, IS THE WAY BLACKNESS IS TRYING AND HAS BEEN TRYING TO EMERGE FROM THE CAGES THAT SOCIETY IS PLACED IT…IT IS TRYING TO EXPLODE OUT AND SAY, LOOK, TASTE AND SEE, THAT I'M GOOD, THE goodness in the fullness. And, you know, it's kind of interesting to take it to an example of expressions of church that I've encountered. I've found myself thinking back to what Black gospel music has meant in much of the church world and how that specific styling of music very much drew upon the experience, some of the sufferings, some of the hope, all of the Black experience to create this particular style and aesthetic, music that resonated with so many more people than just the church, you can now sing a gospel song and people

ANYWHERE IN THE WORLD, REGARDLESS OF WHAT FAITH THEY IDENTIFY WITH CAN RELATE TO THAT FEELING THAT SOULFUL TOUCH, THAT TELLS THEM THAT THINGS ARE GOING TO GET BETTER...THAT THEY'RE GOING TO BE ABLE TO GET THROUGH THIS DIFFICULT TIME. THAT'S, THAT'S JUST MAGICAL. AND I THINK THAT THAT'S JUST A SMALL GLIMPSE OF WHAT, OF WHAT BLACKNESS CAN OFFER.

JEFF HOOD:

WHEN THE SPIRIT GETS LOOSE ON PENTECOST...THERE WERE ALL THESE PEOPLE WHO ARE STANDING THERE SAYING, YOU KNOW, THESE PEOPLE MUST BE DRUNK, THERE MUST BE SOMETHING WRONG, YOU KNOW, JUDGING THEM. THEY'RE TRYING TO EXPLAIN EVERYTHING THAT'S GOING ON. AND WHAT ENDS UP HAPPENING SO OFTEN WAS WITH BLACKNESS, WHEN WE ENGAGE THE SPIRIT OF BLACKNESS, WHEN WE COME ALIVE, WHAT ENDS UP HAPPENING IS PEOPLE WANT TO SAY, WELL, YOU KNOW, THEY WANT TO CREATE ALL OF THESE CAGES OF JUDGEMENT, THESE CAGES OF RHETORIC, THESE CAGES OF ASSUMPTIONS, that doesn't allow the blackness to thrive and to be let loose. I mean, I feel like every time a new form of music, a new way of dancing, a new way of thinking, a new way of being comes about, there's always people who want to say, "Well, you can't do that...you can't say that...you can't be that." It's almost as if the world is determined for the canvas to stay white...is determined for the space to remain normal...to remain mundane. And blackness, pushes back and says, "No! We are going to embrace the spirit as the spirit comes, we are

GOING TO SPEAK NEW LANGUAGES, WE'RE GOING TO DO NEW THINGS, WE'RE GOING TO THRIVE, EVEN IN THE MIDST OF YOUR CAGES, EVEN IN THE MIDST OF YOUR OPPRESSIVE WORDS, YOUR OPPRESSIVE WAYS OF THINKING, WE ARE GOING TO THRIVE." AND BLACKNESS, TO ME IS THE VERY DEFINITION OF WHAT IT MEANS TO THRIVE...TO TRULY BE HUMAN.

YOEL OMOWALE:

I THINK IT'S SO IMPORTANT TO NOT QUENCH THE SPIRIT. IT'S SO IMPORTANT...THE WAY THAT WE'RE

EVEN DOING IT NOW...TO ACKNOWLEDGE THE, THE NAMES AND THE STYLES AND WHERE BLACKNESS COMES. SO THAT WHEN WE ALLOW THESE EXPRESSIONS TO BE CHANNELLED THROUGH US...WE DO SO IN A WAY THAT HONOURS THE GOD FROM WHOM BLACKNESS COMES FROM. IT'S A BEAUTIFUL EXCHANGE. IT'S A BEAUTIFUL ACKNOWLEDGEMENT. IT'S A FORM OF PRAISE. WE MUST TELL THESE STORIES. WE MUST SPEAK THESE TRUTHS. WE MUST TELL OUR TRUTH. FOR SUCH BEAUTY IS THE ONLY THING THAT CAN LIBERATE. SO, WE MUST TELL PEOPLE WHERE THE

BEAUTY COMES FROM...WHERE LIBERATION COMES FROM.

JEFF HOOD:

RIGHT, THERE'S A THERE'S A HISTORY OF RESISTANCE. I MEAN, THERE'S THE SENSE IN WHICH BLACKNESS IS ALWAYS RESISTING WHITENESS. AND AS THE SPIRIT GETS LOOSE IN THIS PENTECOST MOMENT, YOU HAVE PEOPLE WHO ARE RESISTING BLANDNESS, THEY'RE RESISTING THE CAGES, THEY'RE RESISTING. THEY'RE PUSHING FOR BROADER...WILDER DEFINITION.

they're pushing for something, something new, something fresh. And I think that that speaks to this idea that God is Black, that God is constantly pushing us to greater definition and constantly pushing us to greater expression constantly pushing us to greater life, to become more fully alive, to become more fully human. And I think that there's tremendous beauty there, that if we are willing to allow the new languages, the new words, the new expressions, the new ways of life to

COME UPON US, THEN WE TRULY ARE ALLOWING OURSELVES TO BECOME BLACK.

YOEL OMOWALE:

I THINK IT JUST GOES TO SHOW THAT THE PENTECOSTAL EXPERIENCE IS, IS CRUCIAL, TO THIS JOURNEY. IT IS A CONTINUAL, RATHER THAN A HISTORIC ONE-TIME EVENT. IN FACT, THE POSSIBILITIES ARE ENDLESS. THE BEAUTY OF BLACKNESS IS THAT IT'S SO EXPANSIVE....IT HAS SO MANY DIFFERENT WAYS OF REINVENTING ITSELF AND

THE POSSIBILITIES OF HOW THAT CAN IMPACT US AND REVIVE US AND, AND EVOLVE US, SPIRITUALLY SPEAKING, ARE TRULY ENDLESS.

JEFF HOOD:

THE PERSON WHO IS TRULY BLACK IS ALWAYS GOING TO BE A PENTECOSTAL BECAUSE THEY'RE ALWAYS GOING TO BELIEVE THAT THE SPIRIT OF GOD...THE SPIRIT OF BLACKNESS...IS ALWAYS MOVING, SHAKING, EXPLODING AND EXPANDING.

ESCHATOLOGY

COME ALL BLACKNESS.

ALL PRAISES BE TO THE BLACK GOD...WHO WAS...WHO IS...AND WHO IS TO COME.

IN THE BEGINNING..... BEHOLD, WE WERE CALLED UP INTO THE HIGHEST HEAVENS...AND EVERYTHING WAS BLACK. WE WERE NOT AFRAID. WE SIMPLY WERE. CURIOUS, WE QUESTIONED, "WHERE AM I?" THEN, A VOICE LIKE A ROARING LION EXCLAIMED..... "YOU ARE AMONGST THE ANCESTORS. THE PLACE WHERE YOU ARE...IS THE PLACE WHERE YOU ARE FROM." EVERYTHING STOPPED. FOR THE FIRST TIME, WE COULD SEE. THE VOICE GUIDED US.

THEN, WE WERE TAKEN DEEPER. "THE TIME IS NEAR." WE SAW A GREAT BATTLE BETWEEN THE FORCES OF

WHITENESS AND BLACKNESS...THE FORCES OF CANCELATION AND LIBERATION. DESPERATE TO BE COUNTED AMONGST THE LIBERATED, WE CRIED OUT. THEN THE VOICE BOOMED, "...ALPHA AND OMEGA'...WHO IS AND WHO WAS AND WHO IS TO COME..." WE REALIZED THAT WE COULD NOT LOSE. WE SIMPLY NEEDED TO CLING TO THAT WHICH IS BLACK. FOR EVERYTHING THAT IS WHITE WILL BE TURNED TO BLACK. FOR GOD IS BLACK.

THEN, WE WERE TAKEN DEEPER. FROM THE TOP OF THE HIGHEST MOUNTAIN, WE SAW INCARNATION OF

BLACKNESS DESCEND. WE'D NEVER SEEN ANYTHING LIKE IT. THERE WAS "A ROBE, A GOLD SASH, WHITE HAIR, FLAMING EYES, BRONZE FEET, A VOICE LIKE SOOTHING WATERS, SEVEN STARS IN THE RIGHT HAND, A TWO-EDGED SWORD PROTRUDING FROM THE MOUTH AND A FACE THAT SHOWN LIKE THE SUN." BLACKNESS WAS THERE IN ALL GLORY. SHOCKED, WE FELL TO THE GROUND AND WORSHIPPED. THEN, WE HEARD THE MOST BEAUTIFUL VOICE WE'D EVER HEARD, "ARISE MY CHILD. BLACKNESS IS YOURS AND YOU ARE BLACK."

Then, we were taken deeper. "...you have abandoned the love your first love." We could see that we had traveled so far from the blackness from which we came. Why did we erase everything? Why did we think everything had to be white? Why did we destroy who we are? "Remember." We could see the whiteness that we'd fallen from. In the realization of the fall, we were able to grasp the cure...blackness. We had to find ourselves again.

THEN, WE WERE TAKEN DEEPER. "I KNOW YOUR AFFLICTION AND YOUR POVERTY, EVEN THOUGH YOU ARE RICH." WE HAVE SPENT ALL OF HUMAN EXISTENCE NOT REALIZING THAT WE ARE RICH IN OUR BLACKNESS. WE ARE SO AFFLICTED. WE HAVE TRADED THE MEANINGFUL FOR THE MEANINGLESS. WE MUST GO BACK. WE MUST RETURN TO THE BLACKNESS THAT BIRTHED US. "REPENT THEN." THE WAY BACK WAS ALSO THE WAY FORWARD. WE ARE THE LIBERATION. WE ARE BLACK. "TO THE ONE WHO RETURNS I WILL GIVE THEM A FUTURE."

THEN, WE WERE TAKEN DEEPER. "I KNOW YOU THINK YOU'RE ALIVE...BUT YOU ARE DEAD." THERE IS NO LIFE IN WHITENESS. THERE IS NO LIFE WITHOUT SUBSTANCE. THE GLORIFICATION OF WHITENESS IS THE GLORIFICATION OF DEATH. WE WERE MADE TO LIVE IN COLOR. WE WERE MADE TO BE COLORFUL. WERE MADE FROM COLOR. WE ARE RETURNING TO COLOR. THOSE WHO REFUSE TO ACKNOWLEDGE SUCH THINGS ARE ALREADY DEAD. "LOOK, I HAVE SET BEFORE YOU AN OPEN DOOR, WHICH NO ONE IS ABLE TO SHUT." LIFE IS ALWAYS AVAILABLE. THE DOOR OF BLACKNESS

IS ALWAYS OPEN. IF WE WILL WALK THROUGH... "I WILL WRITE ON YOU THE NAME OF GOD...BLACK"

THEN, WE WERE TAKEN DEEPER. THERE ARE THOSE WHO TRY TO BE EVERYTHING TO EVERYBODY. BLACKNESS IS NOT MOCKED. "I KNOW YOUR LIFE...YOU ARE NEITHER BLACK NOR WHITE." WE ARE CALLED TO BE WHAT WE WERE MADE TO BE. WE ARE CALLED TO LIVE HOW WE WERE CREATED TO LIVE. WE ARE CALLED TO MOVE HOW WE WERE CREATED TO MOVE. WE ARE CALLED TO THINK HOW WE WERE CREATED TO THINK. BLACKNESS IS ABOUT FREEING

THE WHOLE PERSON. BUT IF WE RESIST... "I AM ABOUT TO SPIT YOU OUT OF MY MOUTH." WE CAN'T CLAIM TO KNOW BLACKNESS PARTIALLY. WE ARE EITHER BLACK OR WHITE. THERE IS NO FREEDOM IN DENYING WHAT IS...ERASING WHAT YOU ARE.

THEN, WE WERE TAKEN DEEPER. RIGHT IN FRONT OF ME, "...A DOOR STOOD OPEN!" WE WERE HESITANT TO GO IN. THEN, FROM WITHIN WE HEARD, "COME IN, AND WE WILL SHOW YOU WHAT MUST TAKE PLACE." WE KNEW THAT A BLACKENING WAS COMING. THE BEAUTY OF THE INVITATION BECAME CLEAR. "AT

ONCE WE WERE IN THE FULLNESS OF BLACKNESS, AND THERE IN HEAVEN STOOD A THRONE, WITH ONE SEATED ON THE THRONE!" GOD...THE REAL GOD...THE BLACK GOD...STOOD IN FRONT OF US. BILLIONS OF ANGELIC VOICES RESOUNDED IN A SUSTAINED CHORUS, "BLACK, BLACK, BLACK, THE COLORFUL GOD ALMIGHTY, WHO WAS AND IS AND IS TO COME." THEN, WE COULD SEE WHERE ALL THE VOICES WERE COMING FROM. "I LOOKED, AND THERE WAS A GREAT MULTITUDE THAT NO ONE COULD COUNT, FROM EVERY NATION, FROM ALL TRIBES AND PEOPLES AND LANGUAGES, STANDING BEFORE THE THRONE AND

BEFORE THE BLACK GOD." THE VOICES GUIDED US TO A PLACE OF EVERLASTING COMFORT AND PEACE. "...IN THE CENTER WERE SPRINGS OF THE WATER OF LIFE, AND THE BLACK GOD WIPED AWAY EVERY TEAR FROM OUR EYES." THE TEARS HAVE BEEN WIPED AWAY...YET THE BATTLE AGAINST WHITENESS RAGES ON.

THEN, WE WERE TAKEN DEEPER. BEFORE ME, WE SAW THE MOST BEAUTIFUL WOMAN I'D EVER SEEN. AMIDST PAINS OF LABOR, SHE BROUGHT FORTH A CHILD. THE CHILD WAS THE SALVATION OF THE WORLD...THE

DIVINE CHILD OF ALL BLACKNESS. WHITENESS GREW ANGRIER AND ANGRIER...AND SOUGHT TO DESTROY ALL COLOR. FROM THAT MOMENT ON, WHITENESS DEDICATED ALL WHITENESS TO WAGE, "...WAR ON THE REST OF HER CHILDREN." BLACKNESS HAS BEEN FIGHTING BACK EVER SINCE. WHICH SIDE WILL WE BE ON? THE SIDE OF ERASURE OR THE SIDE OF COLOR. THE SIDE OF BLACK OR THE SIDE OF WHITE. MAKE NO MISTAKE. THERE IS A WAR RAGING. WE WILL ALL BE JUDGED..."ACCORDING TO OUR WORKS."

THEN, WE WERE TAKEN DEEPER. BEHOLD, WE SAW THE BEAUTY, "THEN WE SAW A NEW HEAVEN AND A NEW EARTH; FOR THE FIRST HEAVEN AND THE FIRST EARTH HAD PASSED AWAY..." WHITENESS WAS BANISHED FROM THE EARTH. EVERYTHING HAD RETURNED TO IT'S PROPER PLACE. EVERYTHING WAS BLACK. EVERYTHING WAS AS IT WAS IN THE BEGINNING. "SEE, THE HOME OF GOD IS AMONGST BLACKNESS..." GOD IS WITH US! WE DO NOT HAVE TO LOOK ANYWHERE BUT WITHIN. BLACKNESS IS THERE FOR ALL. WHITENESS IS PASSING AWAY. "SEE, I AM MAKING ALL THINGS NEW." GOD IS MAKING ALL THINGS BLACK.

THE UNSEEN HAS BECOME THE SEEN. BLACKNESS IS NOW THE FOCAL POINT. GOD DECLARES, "I AM BLACK...THE ALPHA AND OMEGA...THE BEGINNING AND THE END." FILLED WITH HOPE, WE WERE TAKEN TO A FLOWING FOUNTAIN, "TO ALL WHO ARE THIRSTY I GIVE THIS WATER." WE DRANK...WE DRANK...WE DRANK...AND WE DRANK...FILLED WITH BLACKNESS...AND WE'VE NEVER THIRSTED AGAIN. THE ESSENCE OF EXISTENCE IS WATER...BLACK WATER. INDEED, BLACKNESS FLOWS FROM THE FOUNT OF CREATION...THE FOUNT OF GOD. "WILL YOU DRINK?"

IN THE END... THE EMPTY SPACE WAS GONE. THE NOTHINGNESS WAS GONE. THE IMPOSTERS WERE GONE. WHITENESS HAD BEEN FILLED IN. BLACKNESS WAS HERE TO STAY. "...THERE WILL BE NO MORE WHITE...FOR GOD WILL BE THEIR FILL..." DESPERATE FOR SUCH A MOMENT, WE CRIED OUT, "WHEN WILL THIS ALL COME TO PASS?" "SURELY, I AM COMING SOON." BEFORE THE VISON WAS OVER, WE SHOUTED, "AMEN. COME, ALL BLACKNESS!"

ALL PRAISES BE TO THE BLACK GOD...WHO WAS...WHO IS...AND WHO IS TO COME.

COME ALL BLACKNESS.

ESSAYS

209

WORDS FROM FERGUSON

JEFF HOOD

"Love is going to fuck you up." The ominous words rang out from a woman standing on the street corner. Pointing at me, the woman declared, "You are going to have to die before you can love anybody here." I knew she was right. The prophetess of Ferguson reminded me of all the times I have tried to pretend that I don't carry my own bigotries in life. I knew

THAT LOVE HAD BROUGHT TO THIS CITY OF DEATH,

BUT MORE WAS GOING TO BE REQUIRED OF ME.

THE BRILLIANT ARRAY OF FLOWERS AND COLORS DOES NOT MASK THE FACT THAT MICHAEL BROWN DIED THERE IN A FLURRY OF BULLETS. THE SPOT IS TUCKED WITHIN AN APARTMENT COMPLEX WHERE POOR PEOPLE LIVE. WALKING UP, I DIDN'T KNOW IF I SHOULD BE THERE OR NOT. I STOPPED AND PRAYED OVER THE SPOT. STEPPING TO THE SIDEWALK, I SAT ON THE CURB NEXT TO A WOMAN.

"I hate white people," she offered without any solicitation. Taken aback, I inquired, "Do you want me to leave?" "No, you are the only chance I've got at redemption," she softly spoke through tears. For a few moments, we sat silently. I didn't know what to say. Through the tension, the woman looked at me and asked, "Are you a bigot?" "Yes ma'am," I offered. "We are both bigots then. I guess we can be a salvation to each other," she replied. For the next little while, we talked about the effect that bigotry has on all of us whether we want it to or not. "If there has ever been a time to be honest about what is going on in our own hearts, it is now. I guess it starts with the honesty we offered to each other," she concluded. After concluding pleasantries, I walked back to the car and thought about what had just happened. Our joint sensibilities of self-protectionism had died and for a brief moment we had an honest vulnerable conversation about bigotry. I think we both left having experienced a moment of resurrection. Death and resurrection go together. I guess that ours was a resurrection in Michael Brown.

I don't believe the incarnation of God was a singular event. I believe that God joins us when we open our hearts to love. I walked to the epicenter of the Ferguson protests, W. Florissant Ave. The night was thick with tension, but I felt alive in love. I joined the chants, "Hands up, don't shoot!" With every foot that hit the pavement, I felt like we were growing together in love and honesty. Someone next to me shouted out, "Where the fuck is God in all of this?" One of my dear brothers responded quickly, "Right here with us! Look around at all these colors of folks holding hands and standing together. God is right here with us." Our hearts were moved by each other. The power of God was right there in the people of God.

There truly is no such thing as death without resurrection. The death of Michael Brown continues to grant new life to all who are

WILLING TO OPEN THEIR HEARTS. MAY OUR OWN PURSUIT OF RACIAL JUSTICE AND RECONCILIATION BEGIN WITH THE DEATH OF THE DISHONESTY IN OUR OWN HEARTS AND CONCLUDE IN OUR OWN RESURRECTION WITH THE WILD DIVERSITY OF THE PEOPLE OF GOD.

AN EPISTLE TO THE CHURCH ON THE SEDUCTION OF WHITENESS INTO IDOLATRY

YOEL OMOWALE

ABOUT 3 MONTHS INTO THE INTERNATIONAL COVID-19 LOCKDOWN, 3 WEEKS AFTER GEORGE FLOYDS ALMOST 9 MINUTE LONG ASPHYXIATION UNDER A COPS KNEE ON 'PAY-PER-VIEW' AND THE WORLD ERUPTING IN PROTEST UNDER THE BANNER OF #BLACKLIVESMATTER, THERE WAS A WHITE EVANGELICAL SCRAMBLE TO BE THE LEADING VOICE on yet another national conversation about strained race relations. After seeing a few misfired attempts I remember reluctantly watching the recorded playback of Pastor Louie Giglio, rapper Lecrae and Chick-Fil-A CEO Dan Cathy having an "honest conversation about race and the church" on the 14th of June 2020"

Giglio had this to say about slavery which torpedoed through social media bringing much critique and rebuke while shattering the mask that white evangelicalism has adorned

CONCEALING ITS CONVICTION THAT WHITE PRIVILEGE IS IT'S RELIGIOUS BIRTHRIGHT:

*"WE UNDERSTAND THE CURSE THAT WAS SLAVERY, WHITE PEOPLE DO, AND [WE] SAY 'THAT WAS BAD'. BUT WE MISS THE **BLESSING OF SLAVERY**, THAT IT ACTUALLY BUILT UP THE **FRAMEWORK FOR THE WORLD THAT WHITE PEOPLE LIVE IN AND LIVED IN.**"*

HE EXPRESSED THAT 'WHITE PRIVILEGE' IS DIFFICULT FOR WHITES TO GET THEIR HEAD AROUND AS A TERM TO DESCRIBE THEIR COLLECTIVE ADVANTAGE SO PERHAPS IT MIGHT BE BETTER TO FRAME THE advantage that white people have as a result of slavery as **the white blessing**; the silver lining to the dark cloud of its brutal atrocity.

I think in a rare moment of white evangelical clarity about its inheritance, Giglio told the truth about how white infrastructural advantage has been sanctified and legitimised through religious sentiment and conviction for centuries.

In Giglio's own words, the very framework of the white world, the capitalistic wealth, its

SOCIAL/CLASS HIERARCHY, THE PAST AND CONTINUED EXPLOITATION OF AFRICA, AND THE SO CALLED LAND OF THE FREE AND THE HOME OF THE BRAVE, WAS ALL ESTABLISHED AND FUNDED THROUGH THE MACHINATIONS OF THE TRANSATLANTIC SLAVE TRADE, AND IS WHAT WHITES HAVE LARGELY BENEFITED FROM AT THE EXPENSE OF BLACK AND INDIGENOUS PEOPLE FOR TIME IMMEMORIAL.

GIGLIO IS NO INNOCENT BYSTANDER AND VICTIM OF A CLUMSY CHOICE OF WORDS AS HE MIGHT HAVE SOME CONVINCED SOME OF IN HIS SUBSEQUENT attempted <u>apology</u> under duress, his remarks were viscerally offensive to the souls of many Black folks who descended from enslaved Africans including mine and centered whiteness as the beauty that emerged from the darkness. Further reflection and attempting to navigate through the soul wrenching pain of his remarks led me to the soul-bearing realisation that this is the kind of white radical truth-telling that needs to happen *on purpose* for the church and wider society to grapple with and investigate the ways that

OUR MODERN WAY OF LIFE AND WAY OF UNDERSTANDING OUR WEALTH DISPARITIES ARE INDELIBLY LINKED TO THE HARROWING INSTITUTION OF SLAVERY. SO PERHAPS THERE IS A "BLESSING" IN GIGLIO'S REVELATORY RENAMING OF WHITE PRIVILEGE AS THE WHITE BLESSING.

THE WHITE BLESSING:

I REMINISCE ON THE EVANGELICAL ANTHEM OF THE LOCK DOWN, PENNED BY ELEVATION WORSHIP — THE blessing. Thousands of churches around the world contributed in creating several virtual collaborative recordings of this song that no doubt was a comforting balm to many believers. The lyrical excerpt below explained who were the recipients of this blessing:

"May His favor be upon you

And a thousand generations

Your family and your children

AND THEIR CHILDREN, AND THEIR CHILDREN"

I CAN'T HELP THINKING THAT THIS SONG TELLS US TACITLY WHO WERE THE ONGOING RECIPIENTS OF THE WHITE BLESSING TOO. WHO FOR THOUSANDS OF GENERATIONS HAVE INHERITED THE PROTECTIONS, THE DIGNITY, THE ASSUMED INDIGENOUSNESS OF WHITENESS.

THE TERM BLESSING CONJURES UP MANY IMMEDIATE THOUGHTS AND IT COULD PROVIDE SOME CONTEXT TO CONSIDER IT'S ETYMOLOGICAL ROOTS TO PALPATE

It's discomfort in my imagination as I explore how it applies to the white blessing.

According to etymonline.com the word bless derives from the old english terms *bletsian, bledsian*, which mean "to consecrate by a religious rite, make holy, give thanks," and is also linked to the proto-germanic **blodison* which means to "hallow with blood, mark with blood from the sprinkling on pagan altars.

The white blessing therefore feels like a divine consecration and purification of white supremacy, including the many means it has conferred advantages to those with white skin, through the ritual shedding of the blood of "pagan" Blacks and Indigenous people on the altar of their sacred lands. This viscerally autopsies the hidden anatomy of the "blessing" of whiteness by shining a light on the bloodletting of the Black body as the required sacrifice.

The concept of blessing is also rooted in the biblical narrative that informs the religious and socio-cultural framework of white western societies.

First, a biblical blessing was a public declaration of a favored status with God. This is most certainly echoed by the many ways that whiteness mediated that favoured status through history. Whiteness conveyed the divine stamp of approval, the characters of scripture, especially the key character Jesus was codified as white which functioned to confer the white race with immutable access to all the resources that God created and the

AUTHORITY TO HOARD AND DISTRIBUTE IT AS IT SAW FIT.

SECOND, THE BIBLICAL BLESSING ENDOWED POWER FOR PROSPERITY AND SUCCESS. IN THE SAME WAY, THE WHITE BLESSING SPEAKS OF WHITE POWER, WHITE PROSPERITY AND WHITE SUCCESS.

WHITE POWER:

WHITE POWER IS UNDENIABLY GENOCIDAL BASED ON THE HISTORIC RECORD. A CLOSE EXAMINATION OF WHITE POWER HAS DEMONSTRATED THAT IT HAS USED EVERY CONCEIVABLE AVENUE AVAILABLE TO EXPLOIT, divide and conquer all in the name of accumulating more power at the expense of indigenous life and violating earths sacredness. White power also wagers war on its own constituents as seen with the inter-European, imperial race to "discover" and colonise the world throughout antiquity. In modern times, white power is varied in the way it's constituted and operationalised. Whether that's through white nationalism which seeks to develop and maintain white racial purity and national identity. They hold that whites

SHOULD PRESERVE THEIR MAJORITY IN MAJORITY-WHITE COUNTRIES AND CONSERVE THEIR CULTURAL, POLITICAL AND ECONOMIC DOMINANCE, THEY ARE OFTEN AGAINST INTERRACIAL MARRIAGE, MULTICULTURALISM, IMMIGRATION OF NONWHITES AND LOW BIRTH RATES AMONG WHITES AS THESE ARE PERCEIVED AS THREATS TO WHITE RACIAL PURITY AND SURVIVAL. WHITE POWER IS THREATENED BY THE VERY EXISTENCE OF BLACK LIVES AND THATS WHY IT MEDIATES VIOLENCE AGAINST THE BLACK BODY AS A DUTY, WHICH IS THE MOST COMPELLING EXPLANATORY POWER FOR POLICE BRUTALITY WITH impunity. The xenophobia and anti-immigrant sentiment of white nationalism is again demonstrated by the way white America flexes in the ballot box and engages hostility towards those who are considered hyphenated "Americans" rather than just plain Americans. I'd also argue the low birth rates in white America is probably the driver for the moral anti-abortion emphasis that takes political priority in fight for maintaining white power strongholds and this is mostly observed in the religious context.

ANOTHER MANIFESTATION OF THIS WHITE POWER IS IN WHITE EVANGELICALISM, WHERE WHITE POWER IS EXPLICITLY SANCTIFIED, GOSPELIZED AND IMMUNISED FROM ATTACK:

THIS ITERATION OF WHITE POWER, IS MEDIATED THROUGH THEOLOGICAL GATEKEEPING, WHERE WHITE THEOLOGIANS GET TO ARBITRATE THE BORDERS OF ORTHODOXY AND ORTHOPRAXY BUT THEIR THEOLOGICAL WORK AND CONCLUSIONS ARE SEEN AS CULTURALLY NEUTRAL. THIS SERVES TO EXCLUDE AND MARGINALISE BLACK AND BROWN THEOLOGICAL contributions and faith expressions or appropriate their voices under the guise of diversity but only to serve the advancement of the white evangelical status quo and influence. This stifling of the Black voice within the evangelical landscape is further demonstrated in the race conversation aforementioned featuring Lecrae and Giglio. White power always controls the narrative, decides who sits at the table, defines the terms and even redefines terms based on its own determination of what is suitable and comfortable to white sensibilities. Black Christians are expected to uphold the political priorities of white evangelicalism almost automatically and are expected to champion those loudly to prove our allegiance within the white evangelical power structure. We feel compelled to conceal our true political ideals in order to remain accepted ambassadors to our communities. You might notice how all of a sudden we seemed compelled to criticise government

ASSISTANCE PROGRAMS FOR THE SOCIOECONOMICALLY DISAFFECTED, SUPPORT EXCESSIVE BORDER CONTROL AND RESTRICTION OF IMMIGRATION WITH THE XENOPHOBIC RHETORIC ALL IN SERVICE OF WHITE NATIONALISTIC IDEALS. BLACK PEOPLE HAVE LEARNED TO BE EXPERT ASSIMILATORS IN WHITE SPACES BY SANITISING OUR CULTURE ORIGINS AND EXALTING WHITE CULTURAL SENSIBILITIES WHICH FURTHER STRENGTHENS WHITE POWER. WE WILL ARGUE THAT IN APPEASING AND APPEALING TO THE WHITE NORMALCY IN ALL ARENAS

OF RELIGIOUS EXPRESSION AND LIVING, WE OPTIMIZE THE EFFECTIVENESS OF THE WITNESS OF THE CHURCH. THESE EVEN PLAYS OUT IN HOW BLACK MORAL SENSIBILITIES ARE OFTEN HIJACKED AND UTILIZED TO GARNER AND INTENSIFY WHITE EVANGELICAL POLITICAL POWER AND INFLUENCE. ONLY THE MORAL ISSUES THAT MATTER TO THE WHITE MAJORITY ARE WE DEMANDED TO POLITICISE FOR THE BENEFIT OF WHITE POWER, BUT THE MORAL ISSUES THAT DISPROPORTIONATELY DISAFFECTS MINORITIES ARE CONSIDERED DIVISIVE AND A DISTRACTION FROM THE GOSPEL. THIS IS EXACTLY WHY ABORTION IS uniformly politicised and racial justice is so controversial and divisive in white evangelicalism, racial justice threatens the very heritage and foundation of the entire cathedral of white power.

Tokenized Black gifts and talents are celebrated and bartered in the temple courts when in otherwise good standing, often the centerpiece attraction with high platform visibility for the white gaze, but this utility doesn't tend to earn leadership or decision making power that might upset the power balance.

In this space the black prophetic voice that enables us to speak truth to power and challenge the way that *the white blessing* creates unjust disparities in socioeconomic, judicial and health outcomes, is silenced, frustrated and atrophied. This perhaps partially explains Lecrae's pre-destined failure to theologically engage more courageously on that white platform when he was told about the white blessing of slavery.

Further to this idea of white theological gatekeeping, the gospel mission and social justice towards the needs of the Black communities are deemed mutually exclusive and we are expected to declare that a social justice oriented gospel is heresy when the justice is for our Black communities. This further insulates white power and prosperity from any critique from those who care about social justice which is undeniably in the scope of biblical justice.

WHITE EVANGELICAL POWER IS STARVED OF REASONS TO LAMENT AND CREATES LITTLE TO NO SPACE FOR BLACK LAMENT WHICH LEADS TO AN IMPAIRED CAPACITY TO DEAL HONESTLY AND SENSITIVELY WITH BLACK CULTURAL PAIN AND DISCOMFORT. THIS FAILURE ACCUMULATES AS WHITE GUILT THAT OCCASIONALLY DRIVES THESE WHITE-LED "RACIAL RECONCILIATION" CONVERSATION BLUNDERS.

WHITE PROSPERITY AND SUCCESS:

3 YOU WILL BE BLESSED IN THE CITY AND BLESSED IN THE COUNTRY.

4 THE FRUIT OF YOUR WOMB WILL BE BLESSED, AND THE CROPS OF YOUR LAND AND THE YOUNG OF YOUR LIVESTOCK — THE CALVES OF YOUR HERDS AND THE LAMBS OF YOUR FLOCKS.

5 YOUR BASKET AND YOUR KNEADING TROUGH WILL BE BLESSED.

6 YOU WILL BE BLESSED WHEN YOU COME IN AND BLESSED WHEN YOU GO OUT.

7 THE LORD WILL GRANT THAT THE ENEMIES WHO RISE UP AGAINST YOU WILL BE DEFEATED BEFORE YOU. THEY WILL COME AT YOU FROM ONE DIRECTION BUT FLEE FROM YOU IN SEVEN.

— DEUT 28:3-7

WHITE AMERICA CONSIDERS ITS PROSPERITY A SIGN OF GOD'S DIVINE DECREE AND APPROVAL. IT HAS WOVEN ITSELF IN THE BIBLICAL NARRATIVE, AS A MODERN REINCARNATION OF *THE CHOSEN PEOPLE*. IT ADDITIONALLY IMAGINES ITS WEALTH IS INDICATIVE OF ITS RIGHTEOUSNESS AND THIS IS WHY IT LARGELY valorises its exploits in the world and can casually see the bright side of slavery as a white blessing. The *prosperity gospel* which unsurprisingly has become much more visible in the mainstream, advocates explicitly this idea that the blessing of God maketh rich and spiritualises the goal of the *American dream* as a core tenet of its faith. This compounds the difficulty for those who have inherited a white blessing, to honestly acknowledge, engage and exorcise the flip side of that which is the black curse that they fabricated to make white

BLESSING A REALITY. THE WHITE BLESSING IS SOMETHING THAT YOU'D WANT TO PASS ON TO YOUR CHILDREN AND THEIR CHILDREN, TO GOSPELIZE THE MESSAGE OF GOD'S FAVOUR AND THE BENEFITS OF THAT BLESSING IN EVERY WAY. IT LEADS YOU TO RETELL HISTORY IN WAY THAT SANITISES THE COSTLY SACRIFICE OF THAT BLESSING, TO SCRUB DOWN THE BLOODIED PAGAN ALTARS WHERE THESE BLESSINGS WERE WROUGHT WITH THE BATTERED BLACK BODY AS PAST AND ONGOING PAYMENT. THE WHITE BLESSING IS ALSO BELIEVED TO BE PROTECTED FROM ATTACK AND SCRUTINY. JUST LIKE THE 7TH VERSE OF

DEUTERONOMY 28 PROMISES THE DEFEAT OF THE ENEMIES OF THE BLESSED, WHITE AMERICA CONTINUES TO RESIST ANY EFFORTS TO DEAL HONESTLY WITH THE PLIGHT OF BLACK PEOPLE WHOM THEY HAVE ARBITRARILY DEEMED THEIR ENEMIES, AND WILL CONTINUE TO KNEEL ON THE GANGRENOUS WOUNDS AND DISPARITIES THEY FACE, EVEN AS BLACKS FIGHT BACK FOR COMPLETE LIBERATION.

THE WHITE BLESSING SIMPLY PUT, MEANS THEY BELIEVE GOD HAS MADE IT CLEAR THAT HE IS ON THE WHITE SIDE, THE RIGHT SIDE.

The more I listen to disillusioned Christians of colour, I am starting to see common threads in our point of departure. Christianity was cleverly woven into a dominant culture conservative narrative, where to fit in required you to leave any part of you that wasn't befitting at the door of sanctification. In order to assimilate you were spiritually incentivised to despise anything that wasn't officially sanctioned by the mainline culturally determined doctrine - and that often included you.

Scripture was too often used as a cultural sieve to separate the parts of you that were to be purged on the altar of God's wrath from the parts of you that could be used to advance the empire of church.

We have been conditioned by the devices of religion, media propaganda and twisted history to distrust and hold in contempt the Black experience. This leads one to deny one's own cultural and ethical reality; one's creative potential, to assimilate as the only way to legitimately be, belong and thrive. In

THE END THIS LEADS TO A PSYCHOSIS OF SORTS.....FOR THIS "WORLD" WAS NEVER DESIGNED FOR YOU AND UNTIL YOU RECOGNIZE THAT AND BREAK OUT OF SUCH DELUSIONS AND DENIAL, YOU WILL NEVER BE FREE.

BLACKOLOGY IS THE REMEDY.

THE FREEDOM WE SEEK AND THE DELIVERANCE WE NEED, IS BLACKOLOGY.

SO I BESEECH THE THEREFORE SIBLINGS, BY THE MERCIES OF BLACKNESS, THAT YOU SUBMIT YOUR BODY, MIND AND SOUL TO THE BAPTISM OF

BLACKNESS AND RELINQUISH THE IDOLS THAT

ENSNARE YOU INTO DAMNATION.

BABEL

JEFF HOOD

*WRITTEN SOON AFTER THE JULY 7, 2016 MASS SHOOTING IN DALLAS, TEXAS IN WHICH A LONE GUNMAN NAMED MICAH JOHNSON COOPTED A MARCH AGAINST POLICE BRUTALITY TO KILL 5 POLICE OFFICERS.

WRITING USED TO BE EASY. NOW, NOTHING SEEMS EASY. LEANING IN, I JUST STARE AT THE SCREEN. OCCASIONALLY, I TRY TO TYPE SOMETHING. DESPITE MY DESPERATION TO WRITE, MY MIND IS HELD CAPTIVE TO A FORMER PLACE.

BLOODY FILMS NEVER LEAVE YOU. EVERY IMAGE STICKS. THE OFFICER TOOK HIS GUN AND SHOT ALTON STERLING DEAD. AMIDST THE SCREAMS, PHILANDO CASTILE BLED OUT. EVERYONE WANTED TO TALK ABOUT THEIR LIVES, I COULDN'T GET PAST THEIR

DEATHS. I WASN'T ALONE. WE PUT OUT A CALL. OVER A THOUSAND PEOPLE RESPONDED.

DOWNTOWN DALLAS HAS BEEN THE SITE OF DOZENS AND DOZENS OF RALLIES. OVER THE LAST YEAR, WE'VE REPEATEDLY MARCHED FOR ENDANGERED LIVES. THE RALLY WAS LARGE. WE DIDN'T HESITATE. THE CROWD WAS READY TO GO. THE SPEAKERS WERE READY TO GO. WE WERE READY TO GO. CRIES OF JUSTICE RANG OUT.

IN THE MIDST OF MISERY, GOD IS INCARNATE. WHEN WE BELIEVE ALL IS LOST, GOD SPEAKS FROM THE BONES. THE BONES RISE UP AND LEAD US ON. THEY DID THAT NIGHT.

I WAS NERVOUS ABOUT SPEAKING. WHEN I OPENED MY MOUTH, EVERYTHING SEEMED CLEAR. THOUGH I SPOKE FOR A LONG TIME, PEOPLE HAVE ONLY REMEMBERED ONE PHRASE, "GOD DAMN WHITE AMERICA." THE GATHERED UNDERSTOOD THE ADAPTATION OF JEREMIAH WRIGHT'S INFAMOUS PHRASING. THE MESSAGE OF UNITY WAS SIMPLE. THE

MESSAGE OF LOVE WAS HEARD. WE MUST BECOME ONE. THERE IS NO WHITE AMERICA. THERE IS ONLY AMERICA. VIOLENCE HAS A WAY OF CREATING CONFUSION.

FEAR IS NOT A PART OF FAITH. I DIDN'T CARE. I WAS AFRAID.

SAFETY WAS AT THE FRONT OF MY MIND. THE DALLAS POLICE DEPARTMENT GUIDED THE MARCHERS THROUGH DOWNTOWN WITH TREMENDOUS GRACE.

ON MULTIPLE OCCASIONS, WE STOPPED OR CHANGED ROUTES TO MAKE SURE THAT EVERYONE HAD THE CHANCE TO KEEP UP. I STAYED AT THE FRONT OF THE LINE. IN TIME, I SETTLED INTO THE RHYTHM OF THE MOVEMENT. THROUGHOUT THE MARCH, ANYTHING SEEMED POSSIBLE. LOVE AND JUSTICE WAS WITHIN OUR GRASP. THEN, CONFUSION REIGNED.

DARKNESS WAS ALL JESUS KNEW. THE DISCIPLES PROFESSED THEIR ALLEGIANCE TO HIM. NOW, THEY COULDN'T EVEN STAY AWAKE. UNABLE TO FUNCTION, JESUS CRIED OUT IN FEAR. NO ONE WAS WOKE.

OUR MARCH WOUND THROUGH DOWNTOWN. STOPPING AT THE OLD COURTHOUSE, WE TOOK A MINUTE TO TALK ABOUT THE 1910 LYNCHING OF ALLEN BROOKS. THERE WAS NO DENYING THAT THE MARCH FOR LOVE AND JUSTICE WAS LONG. FOR A FEW SECONDS, I STARED AT THE BRICKS. WHAT DID THEY KNOW? WHAT WOULD THEY SAY? HOW MUCH FURTHER IS THE JOURNEY? ORGANIZERS AND THE POLICE SHOUTED FOR ME TO RUN UP TO THE FRONT OF THE MARCH. I DID.

For the next few blocks, I talked to a DPD major. In the midst of the rally and protest winding down, we talked about the success of the night. The conversation felt natural. There seemed to be a genuine connection. A few steps past Austin St., everything changed.

Things seemed clearer before Babel. Now, no one speaks the same language. Confusion is all anyone knows.

"POP-POP-POP-POP-POP…" I HEARD IT SO CLEARLY. I'VE HEARD IT EVER SINCE. THE SHOTS RANG OUT. THE VIOLENCE WAS ALL THAT WAS CLEAR. BULLETS FLEW IN EVERY DIRECTION. MULTIPLE PEOPLE DROPPED. THE ECHOES ONLY ENHANCED THE TERROR OF IT ALL. PANDEMONIUM TOOK OVER. GRABBING MY SHIRT TO MAKE SURE I HADN'T BEEN SHOT, I RAN BACK TOWARD THE PROTESTORS. I WAS TERRIFIED THAT A THOUSAND PEOPLE WERE ABOUT TO WALK INTO THE MIDDLE OF A SHOOTOUT. THROUGHOUT THE EVENING, I CARRIED A 10-FOOT CROSS. AT THIS MOMENT, I USED IT AS A SHEPHERD'S STAFF AND STARTED SWINGING IT

AROUND. SCREAMING, "RUN! RUN! ACTIVE SHOOTER! ACTIVE SHOOTER! GO! GO!" I GOT AS MANY PEOPLE OUT OF THERE AS I COULD.

THE MARCH WAS BEAUTIFUL. EVERY STEP WAS ABOUT STOPPING VIOLENCE. LOVE AND JUSTICE SEEMED SO LOUD AND SO CLOSE. EVIL DIDN'T LISTEN. 5 OFFICERS WERE DEAD. DEVASTATION SET IN.

TOTAL CONFUSION ARRIVED.

FOR THE NEXT FEW DAYS, I TOLD MY STORY ON EVERY MAJOR NEWS OUTLET IN THE COUNTRY AND BEYOND. THE OFFICERS WERE NEVER FAR FROM MY MIND. REPEATEDLY, I REMINDED PEOPLE THAT THIS WAS A NONVIOLENT PEACEFUL PROTEST. "LOVE" AND "JUSTICE" WERE THE ONLY WORDS ON MY LIPS. I LOOKED DIRECTLY INTO THE CAMERA AND DECLARED, "STOP SHOOTING AMERICA!" I DON'T KNOW IF ANYONE HEARD ME. VIOLENCE ALWAYS CONFUSES THE EARS. I SAW IT HAPPEN. I SAW IT HAPPEN AGAIN IN BATON ROUGE. FORMER WORDS ARE CONFUSED

AND PRESENT WORDS ARE CONFUSING. WE WILL NOT BE ABLE TO UNDERSTAND UNTIL WE STAND DOWN.

OH GOD, DELIVER US FROM BABEL.

AMEN.

THE FALL: *SOOT AND STENCH*

YOEL OMOWALE

A PASSAGE FOR BLACKOLOGICAL ANALYSIS—

'ON A CURIOUSLY CHILLY AUGUST NIGHT IN THE LUSH, STILL PLAINS OF THE YORKSHIRE MOORS, THERE IS A STIFF WESTERLY WIND RUSTLING IN FROM THE HUMID HILLTOPS DRIVING OUT THE UBIQUITOUS CLOUD OF BLACK SMOKE SETTLED ON THE GROUND LIKE A BLANKET OF DEATH. THE GLOWING EMBERS FLICKER as a fading reminder of what just occurred; the ashy ruin that remains lays lifelessly and already tells a tale. The starry sky seems mysteriously quiet in an unusual and ominous way tonight; almost like she offered a premonition. There is definitely a tension in the air, a pregnant reckoning of something forbidden. My sweaty *blackbody* quickens as I awaken, stumbling from a hazy, half-remembered dream. I instinctively hack up a lung trying to clear what almost vividly tastes like soot lingering bitterly on my

TONGUE. THE STRANGE STENCH OF DEATH HOVERS OVER MY LIFELESS *BLACKBODY.* IT'S SEVENTEEN MINUTES PAST MIDNIGHT AND I AM DRENCHED IN A COLD, NERVOUS SWEAT SHUFFLING THE JIGSAW PIECES TOGETHER OF WHAT JUST HAPPENED IN MY DREAM. THE WHISPERS GROW LOUDER, MORE HARROWING, AND PERSECUTORY AS THEY ECHO WHAT EVERY NIGGER HAS EVER BEEN TOLD IS THEIR PLACE IN THIS COLD, WHITE WORLD.

IT SUDDENLY DAWNS ON ME THAT I MISSED A DOSE OF MY ANTIDEPRESSANTS LAST NIGHT AGAIN FOR THE FOURTEENTH NIGHT IN A ROW YET THE ANNOYANCE IS

WARMLY COMFORTED BY THE FACT THAT I CAN GET AN ERECTION MORE EASILY OFF THOSE WRETCHED COCK BLOCKERS. IN A HALF ATTEMPT TO RELIEVE THE KNOTS IN MY INNERMOST BEING, MY BACK ARCHES AS I RELAX MY SHOULDERS, TRYING TO SQUEEZE OUT AN ANTICIPATORY SMILE WHILE ARM WRESTLING THE BELLY-CLINGING BUCKLE OF MY DENIM PANTS. I BEGIN TO DISPASSIONATELY BASH MY FLACCID MANHOOD FOOLISHLY HOPEFUL, BUT QUICKLY

RELENTING TO THE LOUDLY UNSPOKEN TRUTH THAT I WAS UNDESERVING OF PLEASURE.

I FEEL LIKE AN OLD, WEARY, AND FORGOTTEN MAN IN THIS YOUTHFUL, DARK-HUED BODY; FOR PENT-UP RAGE HAS BESET MY SUPPLE JOINTS WITH A RUSTY EROSION, LIKE A GRINDING GRANDMOTHER'S HIP: STIFF, PAINFUL, AND DYSFUNCTIONAL. A KIND OF RAGE THAT DOESN'T BUBBLE UP TO THE SURFACE OF MY BLACK-SKINNED LIPS FOR THE THOUGHT OF ITS VISIBILITY FRIGHTENS ME. IT PICKLES MY BRAIN LIKE FORMALDEHYDE PREPARES MY BLACK MIND AND

BODY FOR BURIAL. THERE IS A CALLOUS, DISABLING NUMBNESS THAT LEADS TO SELF-NEGLECT AND MALNOURISHMENT, A LACK OF ATTENTION TO ANY DETAILS OF THE NEEDS OR DESIRES OF MY BODY, WHICH HAS BECOME A FAMILIAR NORM. I REACH FOR A FINGERPRINT-STAINED GLASS OF STAGNANT WATER ON MY CLUTTERED BEDSIDE TABLE TO QUENCH SOMETHING THAT ISN'T YET CLEAR TO ME. AS I PRESS MY MOISTENED LIPS AGAINST THE GLASS WHICH STEAMS UP UNDER MY BELABOURED BREATHS, I'M STUNNED BY FLASHES OF TRAUMA THAT CONNECT LIKE A HEAVYWEIGHT UPPERCUT; WHAT IS THIS DRIZZLING of sweet revenge that beats the ground like epileptic fits of rage, quickly evaporating from my imagination soon after they arrive? I become almost convinced I've done something that I am not socially permitted to do. There is such a thing as the Negroes prerogative. Our place, our expectations, our particular vices, our limits. Taking one defiant step beyond the policed boundaries of our station is a perilous step too far for the Negro. I have learned through societal indoctrination to conceal my contempt for what is; to ignore the putrid stench of our simultaneously living yet rotting black bodies. We black folk can't help take notice of our corporate condition, while others turn a selectively blind eye. I've studied with clinical precision the way black bodies are both despised and envied, the deep and dark history tattooed in the skin wrapping our bones; yet whenever it's time to protect our dignity and promote our flourishing then pockets get shallow, hands get tight-fisted and we are lectured on the perils of learned helplessness through handouts. We are also often virulent conduits of our own despising; we encapsulate the programmed contempt of our bodies, culture, and spirituality like the mad cow disease that slowly erodes the brains of its unsuspecting victims. It's a peculiar world to be Black where no matter how much money you make, how many letters are stacked in front or behind your name, regardless of your religious performance, your political alliances, or the side of town you live on: you are still just another feckless nigger to many."

The urge to drink comes over me so I stumble through the dimly lit room stepping over old dinner plates with dry half-chewed chicken bones, clattering zigzagged towards the staircase. I inwardly scold myself for the racket knowing I can't wake my children and have their certain harassment to endure. The air gets fresher as I leave my dusty den and slide my fingers down the old Victorian-styled banister towards the cellar. These 200-year-old houses have a haunted feeling, and the smell of damp firewood, the dark walls seem so depressed and hold the secret gossip of black servants only recently emancipated. Rusted bells that decorate the ceiling almost still chime, a reminder that the ghost of the master could beckon at any time. They lived a sort of simple life. Their recently ransomed freedom was wholly invested in the comfort of their white aristocratic employers. The little they earned meant they had to remain working in conditions deleterious to their black bodies and souls in order to survive a society that only tolerated their defiant existence. The ugliness of their quarters was a constant, enclosing reminder of their repellent existence, cramped under the extravagance of their masters home above. I could almost hear their coded conversations of their frustrations yet they were freer than they had ever been before in recent memory. Somehow this wasn't enough to placate their audacious desire for more than they were given.

"Much hasn't changed," I thought as I shrugged indifferently.

I pull open the wine cupboards as their rusty hinges squeal in protest, momentarily gazing at the labyrinthine decor on its peppered oak door. I grab a vintage Bordeaux wine I'd been saving for a day to celebrate that never came; because like Grandma used to say, a good wine was never to be wasted on indulgence. I began reaching for the largest glass I could find when I'm slightly embarrassed by the thought that I hadn't washed my hands after earlier below navel adventures. I ritually rinse my hands to get off any remnant of sin that glistened blue-black in the moonlight filtering through the basement window. I poured myself a glass of wine stiff-lipped, aloof, and began to sip with profound intention. I get philosophical with alcohol especially in excess, yet tonight I feel notably less inspired.

GAZING OBLIQUELY TOWARDS THE WINDOW I NOTICE THE MOON SEEMS MORE DISTANT AND NOT ITS USUAL SELF-GIVING NATURE OFFERING SOMETHING TO VIBE OFF OF. I REACH FOR MY MOBILE PHONE IN MY POCKET TO PLAY WHAT I KNEW WOULD GET THE JUICES FLOWING. IGNORING THE SEVERAL MISSED CALLS FROM MY BOSS, MY THERAPIST, AND MY PASTOR, I PUT ON AN OLD FAMILIAR SONG, THE SULTRY TONES OF NINA SIMONE WHO I CALL THE VOICE OF GOD, AS USUAL PUTS ME IN THE MOOD TO BE FRIGHTFULLY HONEST WITH MY INNER CHILD. SHE MAKES ME SENSUALLY TACTILE, HELPS ME RECOUNT

WHAT I WOULD RATHER FORGET, AND HELPS ME TELL A STORY OF PAIN THAT I'D RATHER ANESTHETIZE. HER VOICE CARRIES ME TO A PLACE OF BOTH DEEP ANGUISH AND ANGER...A SORT OF BITTER COCKTAIL

THAT TASTES LIKE THE FUNERAL PROCESSION OF A BLACK CHILD.

WHAT WAS THAT DREAM ABOUT? THE MUSIC FANS MY CURIOSITY BUT THE FEELING BECOMES ANNOYINGLY FAMILIAR LIKE THIS IS A REGULAR RITUAL OF FUTILITY.

THE ROOM EXPANDS AND I START TO FEEL THE RAGE COME OVER ME AGAIN, MY EYE TWITCHES, COOL BEADS OF SWEAT DRIP FROM MY FURROWED BROWS, AND I REMEMBER THE PICTURES OF ANOTHER POLICE SHOOTING OF AN UNARMED BLACK DISEMBODIED

CARCASS IN THE UNITED STATES. I GET A HEADACHE AS I FLASH FORWARD TO THE RITUALISTIC CRIES FOR FORGIVENESS FROM THE BLACK CHRISTIAN COMMUNITY. I THINK TO MYSELF PERHAPS THAT'S JUST AN AMERICAN PHENOMENON, RACISM AND ITS PERFORMATIVE DENIAL ISN'T A BRITISH PROBLEM, WE ARE MORE CIVILIZED THAN THAT AS I COMB MY COARSE DREADLOCKS NERVOUSLY THROUGH MY SWEATY FINGERS. WE BRITS RESPECT THE RULE OF LAW AND CONSCIENCE. I TELL MYSELF THAT RHETORIC UNCONVINCINGLY AS I NERVOUSLY INDULGE MORE LIQUOR AND BEAT MY CHEST TO EASE THE

HEARTBURN. THERE ARE TWO MAIN BLACK NARRATIVES IN BRITAIN THAT DOMINATE THE SOCIETAL UNDERSTANDING OF OUR PURPOSE AND PLIGHT. BLACK AS A PROBLEM AND BLACK AS THE VICTIM. A STRANGE SEE-SAW BETWEEN EACH DICHOTOMY SPINS THE CURRENT RACIST META-NARRATIVE WHICH IS BELIEVED DETACHED FROM HISTORY AND SIMPLY UNDERSTOOD AS THE CONSEQUENCE OF NATURE'S INEVITABILITY. WE ARE A PROBLEM AND VICTIM OF NATURE ITSELF WHICH EXPLAINS HOW EUROPE WAS ABLE TO JUSTIFY ENSLAVING, DESTROYING OUR CULTURE AND spirituality, and saving our souls through religious exploitation. We abide a nation that used Christian missiology to legitimize their racial prejudice and envy of indigenous people worldwide, giving them religion and taking away their resources as a divinely mandated exchange. Churches were schools of cultural indoctrination for the enslaved to abandon their own spiritual practice to become more like white people for their salvation.

As my eyes continue to capture the ancient oppressiveness of this dark, stuffy basement, I'm almost blinded by this illuminating thought: it's the curse of the Black immigrant to a white nation to always feel like a foreigner even when a fully participating, tax-

PAYING CITIZEN. IT'S LIKE YOUR CONTRIBUTIONS ARE PAYING RENT IN A HOUSE YOU WILL NEVER OWN. NO MATTER HOW MUCH YOU EARN, YOUR LEVEL OF EDUCATION, OR HOW USEFUL YOU ARE, YOU CANT SLEEP WITH BOTH EYES CLOSED FOR FEAR THAT YOU ARE VIOLENTLY AWAKENED TO THE REALIZATION THAT BRITISH CITIZENSHIP DIDN'T MAKE YOU ENGLISH. AS SOON AS YOU TALK ABOUT THIS IN OL' ENGLAND, YOU FACE EXASPERATION AND WHITE FRUSTRATION; LISTENING INTO SUCH MUSINGS REARING TO MINIMIZE, GET DEFENSIVE, OR ENTIRELY DISMISS. THE MOST UNCONTESTED SOCIAL MYTH IN GREAT BRITAIN

IS THE IDEA OF ENGLISHNESS AND WHITENESS BEING SYNONYMOUS. THE RACISM WE FACE RELIES ON THE VALIANT, NATIONALISTIC EFFORT TO ENCAPSULATE BLACKS IN THE PRESENT, TO DENY, REVISE AND ROMANTICIZE THE PAST- ESPECIALLY HOW EVERY MAJOR WESTERN ACADEMIC DISCIPLINE AND INSTITUTION; BOTH RELIGIOUS AND SECULAR, WERE COMPLICIT IN MAKING THE BED OF BLACK SUFFERING.

TEARY-EYED AND SOMEWHAT TIPSY I ASK, "WHY DO I FEEL SO ANGRY AT THE WORLD AND UNABLE TO LET IT out, unable to find an empathetic ear that won't sell me out."

There are very few spaces to be legitimately angry as a Black man in Britain I continued to muse unceremoniously. Certainly none without dire consequence or jaded judgment. Not at work where you are surrounded by white ideals, where white sensibilities are the

ARBITERS OF DECORUM AND WHITE RESPECTABILITY PROHIBITS BLACK INDIGNATION ON EVERY FRONT. ANGER OFTEN EMERGES SUDDENLY AS MY PUREST AND MOST HONEST EMOTION. IT IS ALSO MY UNDOING, YET WE LIVE IN A WORLD WHERE PURITY AND HONESTY ARE CONSIDERED THE PRESUMED BIRTHRIGHT OF WHITENESS. BUT ANGER—BLACK ANGER, INHERENTLY MAKES MY UNDOING DESERVING.

RESPECTABILITY IS THE MASK THAT SO MANY OF US USE OUT OF NECESSITY TO CAMOUFLAGE THE VISCERAL ANGST AND INTERNALIZED SELF DISDAIN THAT SOAKS OUR NEURONS AND COURSES THROUGH our veins. It never heals the festering boils beneath its veneer that becomes exposed when we are alone and naked.

That anger is forbidden at church where religion's primary role is to keep your body and mind subdued and sanctified, contained and restrained, fit for the western exploitation and constantly demonizing our most honest and empirical emotions. We rehearse a religious affirmation of the poisonous rhetoric believed by white people

ABOUT US; WRETCHED SINNERS DEAD IN THE SINS OF OUR ANCESTORS, SEXUAL DEVIANTS, SPIRITUALLY LOST AND IN NEED OF A WHITENED SAVIOUR AND HIS MISSIONARY FOLLOWING. AFTER ALL, WHITENESS, OUR ABILITY TO ACQUIESCE, PERFORM AND ASSIMILATE INTO ITS POWER TO CIVILIZE US IS OUR only redemption in a world governed by its predilections.

We sing freedom songs and hymns while enswathed in economic chains, hoping for what exactly? To bring down Jericho?

Nonetheless, I love the music we muster to soothe the emotional pain we tirelessly endure, but songs don't bring down the walls of this modern-day Jericho. You can sing "Break Every Chain" in every key and in every

CHURCH SERVICE UNTIL YOU ARE BLUE IN THE FACE. UNTIL THERE IS A STRATEGIC TAKEDOWN OF OPPRESSIVE POLITICAL AND ECONOMIC SYSTEMS THAT HOLD THE KEYS TO CERTAIN CHAINS, THEY WILL REMAIN UNMOVED BY THE UNIFIED CHORUS OF BLACK LAMENT. TOO MUCH INJUSTICE AND VICTIM SILENCING HAVE OCCURRED WITH BIBLICAL INJUNCTIONS CONCERNING BLACK FOLK WHICH LEAVES ME AMBIVALENT ABOUT THE TENABILITY OF

CONSERVATIVE RELIGIOUS SPACES FOR BLACK RADICALISM AND LIBERATION IN THIS NATION.

YOU CAN'T BE FREE TO LAMENT AT THE FAMILY HOME BECAUSE BLACK MEN WHO LET THE BLACK CAT OF RACIAL FRUSTRATION OUT THE BAG TAINTS THE INNOCENCE OF CHILDREN, SHATTERING THEIR NAÏVE SENTIMENTAL EXPECTATIONS OF THE BIG WHITE WORLD OUT THERE. THE BIG BLACK MAN FREELY UNDERSTANDS HE IS AN IMPOSING THREAT WHEN ROAMING WHITE STREETS WITH PICKET-FENCED, WELL-MANICURED LAWNS AND GOLD-PLATED TOILETS. HE

FEELS HIS SIZE IS A PRESUMPTION OF DANGER AND DESPERATELY TRIES TO MAKE HIMSELF AS SMALL AS POSSIBLE TO MITIGATE THE HARM ANTICIPATED. HE MIGHT NOT READILY NOTICE THIS THREAT IS OFTEN PERCEIVED IN THE HOME BECAUSE OF HIS RAGE, SO HE WOULD DO WELL TO KEEP A NAKED FLAME OF INDIGNATION SMOKING OUTDOORS.

THE DISPOSITION WE ARE EXPECTED TO PRODUCE IN THE FACE OF WHITE HOSTILITY IS AN ENDURING PATIENCE, NEVER BEGRUDGINGLY, AND A HUMBLE, VIRTUE-SIGNALING GRATITUDE FOR THE opportunity to be here in any condition you find yourself. However, you must never make the erroneous conflation that such an opportunity is an inalienable right, irrespective of how hard you work or what you achieve for this nation or for yourself. We are permanently aware that we could be told to exit like Brexit on the day you show

DISSATISFACTION WITH THE REALITY OF WHAT IT'S REALLY LIKE TO BE BLACK AND BRITISH.

SO YOU INHALE THE CONTEMPT AND ANGER AND IT BEGINS THE PROCESS OF INTERNAL DECAY, YOU BEGIN TO LOSE YOUR GRIP ON YOUR SOUL AND YOUR MIND SLIPS INTO OBLIVION.

I NOTICE MY HEAVYWEIGHT BODY AS IT DROOPS INTO A DRUNKEN STUPOR AND MY INNER SELF DISDAIN BEGINS TO SURFACE TO THE FORE OF MY MIND. THERE IS NOTHING ENGLISH ABOUT ME YET I KNOW ITS

PARAMETERS SO FUCKING WELL. NOT EVEN THE ACCENT I FEIGNED TO ASSIMILATE AND REFINE MY LINGUISTIC AESTHETICS EVER GAVE ME THE SLIGHTEST SENSE OF NATIONAL BELONGING. I'VE PICKED UP SOME OF THEIR LINGUISTIC STRATEGIES THROUGH THE YEARS BY NOT TELLING THE HARD TRUTH ABOUT THE HOSTILITY I'VE FACED THAT HAS EXACERBATED MY DIS-EASE.

FOR INSTANCE, THE ENGLISH ARE MOSTLY KNOWN FOR LINGUISTIC DIPLOMACY AND EUPHEMISM IN THE WAY THEY EXPRESS CONTEMPT FOR ANYTHING,

ESPECIALLY THEIR ETHNIC PREJUDICES. BUT JUST LIKE THE BLACK FOOTBALLER ON THE NATIONAL SQUAD GETS OVERT RACIAL, DEHUMANIZING, AND XENOPHOBIC ABUSE FOR MISSING A CRUCIAL PENALTY, SO IT IS WHEN BLACK FOLKS MISS THE MARK CAUSING WHITE INCONVENIENCE OR EXASPERATION.

THIS IS THE VISCERAL IMPULSE OF BRITAIN WHEN IT COMES TO HOW SHE COLLECTIVELY VIEWS THE BLACK OTHER WHEN WE DROP THE BALL. SHE WANTS THE EXOTIC, SEXUALLY AND PHYSICALLY HIGH-PERFORMING NEGRO TO EARN HER UPKEEP, KICKING

WHATEVER FECKING BALL SHE DETERMINES IS IN THE BEST INTEREST OF THE FLEDGLING EMPIRE. THAT'S THE HISTORY OF THE SENTIMENT OF THIS NATION THAT IS CONCEALED WHEN WE DRIBBLE SUCCESSFULLY. AS LONG YOU LEARN ENGLISH, CULTURALLY ASSIMILATE, PAY TAXES, APPEAR OTHERWISE RESPECTABLE, YOU GET SOMEWHAT SHIELDED BY THE BRUNT OF ABUSE UNTIL YOU FUCK UP JUST ONCE TOO MANY. ALL OF US BLACK FOLKS RECOGNIZE THE FEELING OF FUCKING UP IN GOOD OL' BRITANNIA AND LETTING DOWN THE TEAM, WE RECOIL INSTINCTIVELY LIKE AN ABUSED child anticipating some sort of heavy-handed and disproportionate chokehold.

The wine bottle by now's half-empty so like a philosopher, this prompts me to survey my life reflecting back on when I arrived in this country, the motherland as imprinted in my colonized imagination. I came here for the chance of a better life I thought. I left behind a sort of lukewarm naivety, having never been to Europe before leaving Jamaica the land of my birth. In Jamaica nothing was beyond my aspirations or personal ambitions, nothing was remotely ordinary either. Everything was loud and in a vibrant rhythm. Everyone that mattered to me, looked like me. We didn't all get along and our nation had its own notorious problems, but I wasn't aware that my Blackness would be controversial and a threat to a white European status quo. I boarded that one-way ticketed plane seat skinning teet' and brimming with every ounce of Jamaican bravado and courage. I must explicitly state that Blackness wasn't

Something I really intimately understood prior to my arrival to this nation. I didn't need to see myself as an abstraction, a colour from the spectrum, or perhaps all of them combined. The Jamaican bravado aforementioned was tied to a rich, cultural experience that backed it up.

I didn't need to exhaustingly explain my dialect to get by, nor did I have to endure being fetishized as exotic because of my skin colour or accent. My blackness prior to immigration was invisible but perfused all of me. In many ways, I miss this pre-awakened naivety and obliviousness I had in the state of this invisible blackness. There was nothing to perform, nothing to prove in my conscious mind at least, and I had to give that up for something I had no preparation for.

Black visibility was something I got baptized into, an almost pentecostal experience, and a very rude awakening. I witnessed the newborn anxiety of now having to explain what was

ONCE INEXPLICABLE. I HAD TO GROW UP QUICKLY TO FIT INTO THE OVERBEARING COSTUME OF BLACKNESS THAT I WAS FORCED TO WEAR BECAUSE OF WHITE ANXIETY AROUND ME. FINDING ANOTHER BLACK FACE ROAMING THE STREETS OF YORKSHIRE BROUGHT A MOMENT OF WELCOME RELIEF USUALLY GREETED BY A BRIEF NODDED AFFIRMATION OR AN ANIMATED SMILE DEPENDING ON THE MOOD AND CLIMATE. IT WAS LIKE WE INSTANTLY KNEW EACH OTHER'S LIFE EXPERIENCES JUST ON THE BASIS OF OUR HUE — THE HILLS AND VALLEYS, AND COULD SING FROM THE SAME ANTIQUE SHEET MUSIC, THE BLUES ABOUT WHAT IT MEANT TO BE black in Britain. I had dazzling glimpses where I unwittingly perceived that what was disdained in much of the dominant culture about Blackness as ugly, was more beautiful than I could ever imagine. This beauty wasn't perfect like whiteness implicitly claimed to be, nor was it homogeneous, permitting one to find one's own niche, one's own voice, one's own catechism. Blackness is a body politic, a social orientation, a liberation struggle, a kind of existential rhythm that I had to come to learn was internationally embraced wherever darker-skinned people happened to find themselves oppressed by those deemed socially white. One thing is for certain, the unifying solidarity of Blackness is so much more than the shade of one's complexion.

Coming to the UK as a teenager literally changed my world and challenged my core conceptualizations of personal and cultural identity. I very quickly discovered something was different enough about me to arouse suspicion. I had to assimilate into white expectations to excel which meant the ambitions I carried were rather bold for my station. Even UK-born Black kids thought I was a little too uppity for their conditioned expectations. I loathed the ways I had to underplay ambition to earn the trust of the coolest kids, and I had to pretend to be an American rap connoisseur, emulating bars I didn't care for, to get the attention of girls and be the cool kind of Black. There was always the regularly featured question of why I chose to leave Jamaica to come to

England and did we all live in mud huts with outdoor toileting facilities. The irony for me there was when my mother grew up in London in the 50's she had an outdoor toilet and my dad who grew in Jamaica around the same time had luxurious indoor toleting.

I staggered my eyes about the room nervously in search of something that might anchor me to reality. The haziness from the liquor and the kind of dreamlike state has made me feel uneasy and queasy. I had a flashback of the night

TERRORS THAT KEPT ME UP LAST NIGHT AS BEING OFF MY PSYCH MEDS CAUSES THESE HORRIBLE WITHDRAWAL PARTIAL DREAM STATES WHERE I FEEL LIKE I AM BEING CHASED BY HOODED KLANSMEN.

WHITE TEACHERS WERE ESPECIALLY UNAFRAID TO REMIND ME OF MY PLACE AT SCHOOL, I NEARLY HAD MY AMBITIONS ASSASSINATED BY MY LESS THAN IMPRESSED WHITE CHEMISTRY TEACHER. HE LOOKED AT ME AS IF I WAS A STRANGE WART WHEN I ATTENDED MY FIRST CLASS AND WITH A TONE MARKED BY CONDESCENSION, ASKED ME WHAT WAS MY CAREER ambition. I told him excitedly I wanted to be a medical doctor, expecting more enthusiasm than what ensued like a gullible child. He looked me square in the face and started to laugh, then remarked matter of factly: "If you became a doctor, I would never let you touch me with a bargepole."

I became that doctor after a long and arduous journey but deep down I've always felt strangely unworthy to touch white patients and haunted by the feeling they all agreed with the bastard's contempt of me. I've never felt I had permission to really be angry about this exchange, I was expected to see this as the rite of passage of a nigger. There had to be a line in the sand circumscribing the white determined limits beyond which we shouldn't trespass. Enduring whiteness and surviving the ways it demands one to ritually purify their Blackness under the tutelage of white normalcy. Why should white patients want me to touch their perfect bodies lest I contaminated them with my contagious and

CONTEMPTIBLE BLACKNESS? HOW MUCH MORE DO I NEED TO EXCEL AND PERFORM TO PROVE I AM JUST AS GOOD AS MY WHITE COLLEAGUES? IF I EVER FUCK UP WILL I BE THE SCAPEGOAT WHO HAS TO TAKE THE FALL FOR THE TEAM? THESE ARE THE HAUNTING QUESTIONS THAT WOULD WHIP MY CONSCIENCE RAW AND BLOODIED BUT NINA SIMONE, COMFORT MY MIND, SOUL AND BODY.

I REACH FOR THE BOTTLE TO POUR ANOTHER GLASS AND ALMOST PREDICTABLY I PASS POINT, KNOCKING THE BOTTLE WITH MY WRIST, AND IN HELPLESS

HORROR WATCH IT FALL SLOWLY TO THE GROUND CLENCHING MY SWEATY PALMS TIGHT AS I ANTICIPATING THE FRACTURING. THERE ARE NO REAL PRIZES IN THIS LIFE FOR NEGROES. JUST STRUGGLE, DISAPPOINTMENT, AND MORE PAIN. ALL GAINS EITHER GO TO THE TAXMAN OR YOU LOSE THEM ALL TRYING TO ASSIMILATE WHILE NEVER TRULY BEING ACCEPTED. THE BOTTLE SMASHES INTO A MILLION PIECES AS IT HITS THE FLOOR BUT I'M TOO INEBRIATED TO REALLY care, but I can't help but notice it's the quintessential metaphor of my life.

I light a Cuban and blow a large ring of smoke into the air while trying to emulate Boris Johnson's voice saying.

"Sing on the stage for us, entertain us, wait on us, clean for us, nurse us and even marry us…give us that exotic service we know you can.. but know your place and your role, we'll take it from there.'"

To understand the current racial dystopian nightmare of Britain it's helpful yet excruciating to reflect back on the not too distant past. As it's been said, history doesn't repeat itself but it most certainly rhymes. At this point, I'm drunk enough to be rendered unable to read the time on the old grandfather clock peering hauntingly in a darkened corner of the room but sober-minded enough

TO PIECE TOGETHER FRAGMENTS OF WHAT OLD RELATIVES WOULD SAY ABOUT WHAT THE '60S AND '70S WERE LIKE FOR BLACK FOLKS IN THE UK. AN OLD NEWSPAPER CUTTING ABOUT CONSERVATIVE MP ENOCH POWELL IN AN OLD SCRAPBOOK ABOUT IMMIGRATION CATCHES MY EYE. IN HIS FAMOUS "RIVERS OF BLOOD" SPEECH IN BIRMINGHAM, ENGLAND 1968; HE RECOUNTED A CONVERSATION with one of his constituents, a white middle-aged working man saying:

"If I had the money to go, I wouldn't stay in this country... I have three children, all of them been through grammar school and two of them are married now, with family. I shan't be satisfied till I have seen them all settled overseas... In this country, in 15 or 20 years'

TIME, THE BLACK MAN WILL HAVE THE WHIP HAND OVER THE WHITE MAN."

POWELL WENT ON TO SAY:

"HERE IS A DECENT, ORDINARY FELLOW ENGLISHMAN, WHO IN BROAD DAYLIGHT IN MY OWN TOWN SAYS TO ME, HIS MEMBER OF PARLIAMENT, THAT THE COUNTRY WILL NOT BE WORTH LIVING IN FOR HIS CHILDREN. I SIMPLY DO NOT HAVE THE RIGHT TO SHRUG MY SHOULDERS AND THINK ABOUT SOMETHING ELSE. WHAT HE IS SAYING, THOUSANDS AND HUNDREDS OF

THOUSANDS ARE SAYING AND THINKING — NOT THROUGHOUT GREAT BRITAIN, PERHAPS, BUT IN THE AREAS THAT ARE ALREADY UNDERGOING THE TOTAL TRANSFORMATION TO WHICH THERE IS NO PARALLEL IN A THOUSAND YEARS OF ENGLISH HISTORY. WE MUST BE MAD, LITERALLY MAD, AS A NATION TO BE PERMITTING THE ANNUAL INFLOW OF SOME 50,000 DEPENDENTS, WHO ARE FOR THE MOST PART THE MATERIAL OF THE FUTURE GROWTH OF THE IMMIGRANT DESCENDED POPULATION. IT IS LIKE WATCHING A NATION BUSILY ENGAGED IN HEAPING UP ITS OWN FUNERAL PYRE. SO INSANE ARE WE THAT

WE ACTUALLY PERMIT UNMARRIED PERSONS TO IMMIGRATE FOR THE PURPOSE OF FOUNDING A FAMILY WITH SPOUSES AND FIANCÉES WHOM THEY HAVE NEVER SEEN."

I ANGRILY FURROW MY BROWS AND CLENCH MY FISTS WITH VIOLENT INTENT AND THINKING TO MYSELF OUT LOUD.

"ONE CAN'T BEGIN TO UNDERSTAND THE INEXTRICABLE RACIST ROOTS AND WHITE NATIONALISM THAT UNDERPINS PERVASIVE ANTI-immigrant sentiment in this country and brexit is only the next chapter in this ongoing saga. yet in spite of this black people are "overreacting" when we express frustration about the continued hostility this exacts on us in particular."

migrants fleeing ex-colonies of britain were the first to come to her rescue after the war and the white populace was frightened by the waves of black and brown faces diluting her culture and racial purity. no one believes

Black Britons, even those who were born here, who report heightened racial hostility since Brexit. The bottom line is this I thought, I will never be considered a "decent, ordinary fellow Englishman" even if I became knighted after saving the Queen's life. As I think about Powell, I can't help to think about my mothers parents, who docked in London on the ship: Empire Windrush looking to help Britain rebuild in the ruins circa 1948. They were given the chilling reception of old fashioned colonial contempt and hardship, despite my

GRANDFATHER DOING WHAT HE COULD TO HELP CHANGE ATTITUDES THEN, HE RETREATED TO JAMAICA WITH HIS FAMILY AFTER REALIZING THAT ANGER FROM HAVING TO ENDURE HEARING HIS DAUGHTER — MY MOTHER, BEING CALLED AN UGLY NIGGER MONKEY, WOULD LAND HIM IN JAIL. BUT MOST OF HIS FRIENDS DIDNT HAVE THE LUXURY TO FLEE, THEY REMAINED AND CHOSE THE SUFFERING HERE AS THEY FELT TRAPPED BETWEEN A ROCK AND A HARD PLACE.

THE WHITE MIDDLE-AGED WORKING MAN WHO EXPRESSED HIS FEAR ABOUT BEING UNDER THE WHIP of the Black man says so much about the psyche of whiteness. It projects its own malevolent predilections onto others as universal, as if it's reasonable to expect that Black people would want to oppress white people if the tables were turned. Black people by large just want the same things everybody else wants in this world: justice and equal opportunity.

At some level, much of the unrest we experience within and witness around us is a manifestation of white collective paranoia about change. That's what drives national politics; primitive fears about the changing demographics, as more brown faces threaten white resources, as queer people demand marriage equality, as women stand tall in a world engineered for and by men. White men are afraid they will be forced to surrender the whip they have benefited from to a darker, less deserving mutiny. There will always be a push and a pull between elements within the dominant majority and pivotal change

NECESSITATED BY THE SLOWLY RISING TIDE OF JUSTICE FOR THE MARGINALIZED.

THE DAY INEVITABLY ARRIVES, LEAST EXPECTEDLY, THAT YOUR BODY CAN'T CONTAIN THE PRESSURE OF THE CONSTANT CONDESCENSION, DERISION, HYPERCRITICISM, AND UNFAIR DEMANDS TO OUT-PERFORM YOUR WHITE COLLEAGUES BEFORE YOU ARE TAKEN SERIOUSLY. MUCH ISN'T EXPECTED OF YOU IN THE FIRST PLACE TRUTHFULLY, SO YOU SPEND TIME FLYING YOUR CONSPICUOUS BLACK ARSE BELOW THE RADAR. BUT WHEN THAT DAY COMES, YOU CAN'T

PREDICT WHAT YOU MIGHT DO. THE ANGER YOU FEEL IS SO FORBIDDEN, SO CURSED AND YOU ARE EXPECTED TO INTERNALIZE THIS AND LET IT WRECK YOU THROUGH A BLACK VICE, AND BECOME ANOTHER BLACK STATISTIC.

IT'S BEEN 100 DAYS AND I'VE AWAKENED TO THIS RECURRING DREAM THAT I CAN'T QUITE DISTINGUISH FROM REALITY. CALM, COLLECTED AND PROFESSIONAL WHITE MEN SURROUND ME DONNED IN WHITE CAPES. THE KIND OF CAPES I ONCE DONNED IN MY DAYS AS A MEDICAL STUDENT I CONSIDERED. THE

MOST FRESH-FACED AND TIMID ONE GRABBED A PLASTIC BOARD FROM THE TABLE IN MY ROOM. HE SEEMED PERPLEXED AND FRUSTRATED, AS IF HE WAS ABOUT TO CHASE OUT TO THE HALLWAY IN AN EMOTIONAL SCRAMBLE BUT HELD HIMSELF TOGETHER. HE WAS HANDSOME, FRIGHTENINGLY SO, AND ON CLOSER INSPECTION, HE APPEARED TO BE MIXED WITH SOMETHING, THERE WAS AN EXOTIC FLAIR TO HIS OTHERWISE WHITE ADJACENT APPEARANCE. HE READ ALOUD RELUCTANTLY A SUMMARY OF WHY I WAS IN THIS STRANGE UNFAMILIAR PLACE AND THE FUTILITY OF MY STAY SO FAR. I HAVE NOT UTTERED A WORD IN

SILENT DEFIANCE TO THESE MEN, TO ANYONE SINCE BEING COMMITTED. I SAID EVERYTHING I EVER WANTED TO SAY THAT FATEFUL, FIREY DAY. THE COLLECTIVE RAGE OF A HUNDRED THOUSAND MALE SLAVES POSSESSED MY BODY, CHANNELING THE UNEXPRESSED FRUSTRATIONS THEY FELT THEY HAD NEITHER THE AGENCY NOR OPPORTUNITY TO RELEASE. IT SOUNDS LIKE I SNAPPED THAT DAY, I TOLD THE WORLD A FEW THINGS THEY NEVER ANTICIPATED FROM A NIGGER THAT THEY ENTRUSTED THEIR PROXIMITY TO. I RUBBED SHOULDERS WITH THE BEST

OF THEM, BUT BY THEN BALDWIN'S PROPHECY OF THE FIRE NEXT TIME HAD COME TO PASS.

REACCLIMATED WITH AN INTOXICATING RAGE.

I CAN FEEL ITS DESTABILIZING TREMOR.

A VENOMOUS FLAVOUR RELEASED AS MY DESICCATED TONGUE PRESSES ONTO THE CRACKED ROOF OF MY MOUTH.

CHOKED UP, WITH REDDENED EYES OF FIRE,

LANGUISHING IN A FEVER OF THE SOUL.

BLOODSHED BRINGS MY BLOOD TO BOIL,

A SLOW SIMMER.

ANOTHER LIFELESS, BLUE-BLACK BODY, GLOWING IN THE MOONLIGHT OF WHITE SUPREMACY AND CASTING ITS HAUNTED SHADOWS ON MY FRAGILE MIND.

A MIND NOW BURSTING AT THE SEAMS, ABOUT TO FRACTURE.

I AM UNDONE.

SCRAWLED ON MY NOTEPAD WERE SOME OF WHAT I TOLD THE WORLD, WHAT I WROTE DOWN AS I DROPPED A MATCH ON THE KEROSENE-SOAKED CARPETS OF THE FALSE REALITY I ABODE. WHATEVER I WROTE ANNOUNCED THAT MY VALIANT EFFORTS TO appease white respectability were expired. This was the other side of performing for the acceptance and applause of whiteness. The illusion of personal progress was shattered and unceremoniously replaced with a diagnosis of despair. I could no longer impress white people with the facade of perfection nor the unfair burden that their

MISTAKES WERE A SIGN OF HUMANITY BUT MY MISTAKES A SIGN OF INCOMPETENCE.

I TOLD THEM I'VE ABIDED ENOUGH RELIGIOUS AND WHITE HEGEMONY FOR ONE LIFETIME, GIVING NOTICE ON TRYING TO NEGOTIATE THE WORTH AND ACCEPTABILITY OF MY OWN COURAGEOUS SPIRITUALITY AND BLACKNESS IN EITHER LATTICE OF LIMITATIONS.

I ANNOUNCED THAT IF THEIR RACIST OR RELIGIOUS EXPECTATIONS OF ME LEAVES THEM DISAPPOINTED IN

MY ANGER, THEN THEY NEEDED TO DROP THOSE EXPECTATIONS. IT WAS NOW CLEAR THAT I WAS NO LONGER ABLE TO APPEASE WHITE CULTURALLY INDOCTRINATED PREFERENCES ABOUT DECENCY AND RESPECTABILITY. I MADE THEM LISTEN TO THE MADDENING REVELATION THAT LIVING AS BLACK AND DISEMBODIED IN ENGLAND IS SOUL-DESTROYINGLY VIOLENT, AND IT TAKES WAY TOO MUCH ENERGY TO convince myself another day is worth living in this suffocating cesspool.

To the colour-blind and indifferent types, I explained, if racism doesn't highly enrage you then that's unsurprising. It likely means you are unaffected by the reliable way it works, the burden it exerts on one's soul. It may not exist in your parameters of reality and for that, I guess you are exceedingly fortunate and to be envied. I reassured them of freedom and privilege to be indifferent and unmoved by

THE INTERNAL SHIVER AND SOCIAL ANXIETY WE FACE BUT TO BE FULLY AWARE THEY ARE COMPLICIT IN OUR SUFFERING.

WITH THOSE WORDS, THE FIRE CONSUMED MY LUNGS LIKE THE GRENFELL TOWER IN LONDON LIT UP THE 2017 SUMMER SKY, AND A THICK VOLCANIC CLOUD OF BLACK SMOKE EMERGED FROM MY LIPS WITH APOCALYPTIC FLAIR AND DISTURBING VIOLENCE.

THERE WAS A VIRTUAL AUDIENCE, OF MOSTLY WHITE GAZE THAT STOOD IN JAW-DROPPED DISBELIEF.

PEOPLE HAVE COME TO FEAR ANGRY BLACK PEOPLE BECAUSE THEY LIVE IN A SOCIETY THAT HAS BENEFITED FROM THE BANKROLLED, STATE-SANCTIONED, CIVILIAN-ENDORSED DEMONIZATION, COLONIZATION, EXPLOITATION, AND GENOCIDE OF OUR ANCESTORS, THEFT OF THEIR LANDS OF ORIGIN; AND ARE REASONABLY PETRIFIED OF WHAT BLACK PEOPLE MIGHT DO WHEN ENOUGH OF THEM AWAKEN

TO THIS REALITY AND ARE FED UP OF BEING TREATED LIKE THE CRIMINALS THEIR WHITE ANCESTORS WERE.

"HE IS CRAZY." THEY SHRUGGED, THE BEST WAY TO DISMISS ENGAGING WITH THE INCONVENIENCE OF MY VULNERABLE RAMBLINGS.

THEY THOUGHT IN BEWILDERMENT AND REPLIED,

"THIS IS THAT BLACK RAGE OUR ANCESTORS FOREWARNED OF THAT THEY SPENT THEIR STOLEN

WEALTH DESPERATELY TRYING TO SUPPRESS. THE DIAGNOSIS IS BLACK APOPLEXY'"

BECAUSE WE WON'T TELL THE BLAZING TRUTH ABOUT OUR NATIONAL CONSCIENCE PERTAINING TO RACE, SO MOST ARE FROZEN IN THEIR ANCIENT RACIAL FANTASIES WHILE OTHERS REMAIN TORMENTED IN A HELLISH RACIALIZED NIGHTMARE.

WHITE CHRISTIANS ARE THEOLOGICALLY COMPROMISED

JEFF HOOD

THESE ARE CRAZY TIMES. FOLK DON'T KNOW WHAT TO DO...ESPECIALLY WHITE FOLK. WITHIN THE WHITE FOLK ARENA, THERE IS ONE GROUP THAT SEEMS TO HAVE LOST ALL SENSE THEY MIGHT EVER HAVE HAD ON REALITY...WHITE CHRISTIANS. ON THE DAILY, I'VE BEEN BOMBARDED BY BIZARRE STATEMENTS/ACTIONS THAT

WHITE CHRISTIANS ARE MAKING/TAKING IN THE NAME OF HELPING. THESE BOMBARDMENTS PROVIDE A TEXTBOOK EXAMPLE OF WHAT THINGS LOOK LIKE WHEN HELPING HURTS. I'VE TRIED TO REFRAIN FROM HAVING THIS CONVERSATION. INITIALLY, I DISMISSED WHITE CHRISTIANS AS HARMLESS...THEN...I STARTED READING THEIR THEOLOGICALLY COMPROMISED BULLSHIT.

"THERE ARE NO WHITE PEOPLE IN THE BIBLE. TAKE ALL THE TIME YOU NEED WITH THAT."

JUST TODAY, I SAW/HEARD THIS QUOTE AT LEAST A DOZEN TIMES. EACH TIME I ENCOUNTERED IT, I THOUGHT ABOUT SOMEONE SEEING IT, THINKING IT WAS CLEVER AND EXCITEDLY SHARING IT. OF COURSE, THIS IS HOW DUMBASSTICITY SPREADS...AND IT IS FAR MORE DEADLY THAN ANY VIRUS.

THINK ABOUT WHITENESS LIKE THIS...

"*TOO MANY* BELIEVE IN THE REALITY OF 'RACE' AS A DEFINED, INDUBITABLE FEATURE OF THE NATURAL

WORLD. RACISM—THE NEED TO ASCRIBE BONE-DEEP FEATURES TO PEOPLE AND THEN HUMILIATE, REDUCE, AND DESTROY THEM—INEVITABLY FOLLOWS FROM THIS INALTERABLE CONDITION. IN THIS WAY, RACISM IS RENDERED AS THE INNOCENT DAUGHTER OF MOTHER NATURE, AND ONE IS LEFT TO DEPLORE THE MIDDLE PASSAGE OR TRAIL OF TEARS THE WAY ONE DEPLORES AN EARTHQUAKE, A TORNADO, OR ANY OTHER PHENOMENON THAT CAN BE CAST AS BEYOND THE HANDIWORK OF MEN. BUT RACE IS THE CHILD OF RACISM, NOT THE FATHER.'"

-TA-NEHESI COATES, BETWEEN THE WORLD AND ME (7)

WHITE IS NOT AN INDUBITABLE FEATURE OF THE NATURAL WORLD.

WHITE IS A MODERN CONSTRUCT.

WHITE IS A SICKNESS.

WHITE IS A CHILD OF RACISM.

WHITE CONTINUES TO BE AND WILL FOREVER BE RACIST...BECAUSE WHITE WAS CREATED TO OPPRESS.

"THERE ARE NO WHITE PEOPLE IN THE BIBLE. TAKE ALL THE TIME YOU NEED WITH THAT."

THOUGH WHITE PEOPLE CREATED MANY OF THE MODERN CATEGORIES OF RACE...THEY DON'T GET TO PUT THAT CONSTRUCT INTO AN ANCIENT TEXT AS IF THE WRITERS WOULD HAVE HAD ANY IDEA OF SUCH A

CONSTRUCT. IT IS YET ANOTHER MANIFESTATION OF RACISM/UNLEASHED MODERNISM.

ON THE OTHER HAND... WHILE IT IS TRUE THAT THERE ARE NO WHITE PEOPLE IN THE BIBLE, THE STATEMENT IS MISLEADING. THERE ARE NO WHITE PEOPLE BECAUSE THE CONSTRUCT OF WHITENESS AS A RACIAL CATEGORY DID NOT EXIST. THE RISE/RACISM OF COLONIALISM CREATED MORE AND MORE OF A NEED FOR PEOPLE OF FAIRER COMPLEXION TO USE THE RACIST CATEGORY OF WHITE. WITH THAT SAID,

Taking white people out of the Bible is also problematic.

White Christians just don't need any more encouragement to separate themselves from biblical moral principles. They have been successful enough at that already. In fact, I believe we must always make sure that white people understand that the oppressors/marginalizers/haters in the scriptures are their kin folk no matter whether they are their skin folk or not.

A BLACK BENEDICTION

...AND NOW MAY THE PEACE THAT SURPASSES ALL UNDERSTANDING GUARD YOUR HEARTS AND MINDS IN THE FULLEST INCARNATION OF BLACKNESS.